Atmamun

Atmamun

*The Path To Achieving The Bliss Of The Himalayan Swamis.
And The Freedom Of A Living God*

Copyright © 2016 Kapil Gupta

ALL RIGHTS RESERVED, no part of this book may be reproduced or transmitted in any form or by any means, electronic or mechanical, including photocopying, recording or by any information storage and retrieval system without permission in writing from the author.

www.KapilGuptaMD.com

www.SiddhaPerformance.com

www.Atmamun.com

Published April 2016

ISBN-13: 978-1532762727
ISBN-10: 1532762720

Book Cover Design by JD&J Design LLC

The moment that man gains freedom from his mind, he becomes a living, breathing God!

— Kapil Gupta, MD

CONTENTS

Introduction	1
What Is Atmamun?	3
What Is The Mind?	10
Why Worship A God?	19
Become God Or Give Yourself To One	23
The Price To Attain God	31
Your Manufactured Self	39
Is Your Life Really A Life? Really?	56
Life Is The Ultimate Absurdity	65
Why Your Life Is Filled With Pain	73
Human Beings Were Not Meant To Be Workers	78
Become A Legend In Your Field	86

The Burden Of Thought	99
Mindfulness Binds. Mind*Less*ness Liberates.	106
No-Mind: The Gateway To Atmamun	111
Meditation: What You've Never Been Told	117
World Peace Is A Cop Out	121
Parents Do Not Raise Children	124
You Are Fast Asleep	140
You Have Everything. But Do You Have Peace?	143
Happiness Will Make You Miserable	156
Bliss In An Instant	159
All Conflict Is Self-Conflict	169
The Rich Man's Greatest Luxury	173
Become The God Of Your Own Life	177

INTRODUCTION

I am not a theist. Or an atheist. I'm not any kind of "ist."

Man was not made to belong to a group. Nor is he strictly an individual. For the concept of an 'individual' can only exist when there simultaneously exists the concept of a 'group.'

Is there a God? Isn't there a God? Why are we here? Is there life on other planets? Most people consider such questions to be important. I say that such questions are asked in order to avoid asking the real questions.

There is pain and risk in asking real questions. Intellectualization is risk-free.

In this book, I've explored and dissected what I believe to be the real questions. Issues that are fundamental to our daily existence. And ones that have the power to transform the life of a human being.

This book is for the True Seeker. This book is for the one who is Sincerely Searching. This book is for the one who has understood that organized religion, self-help, new age, and motivational vehicles are meant for entertainment rather than Transformation.

Atmamun is a path to becoming the God of your own life.

It is the path to achieving outright bliss. It is the path to achieving unbridled freedom.

Atmamun is a path which leads to the bliss experienced by the Kings of human civilization: The Himalayan Swamis.

Atmamun is a path which leads to uncompromising freedom in every possible way.

Man cannot be free until he realizes how deeply he is bound. He cannot use his mind until he first breaks free from its control.

Together, we will work through this person you call "yourself" in order to get to the You that lives behind him.

Together, we will explore the truth behind the ideas and the philosophies that society has filled you with.

In dissecting the major questions about life, the fundamental nature of mind, and in exploring the different roles that human beings assume, you will begin to shed false notions. And drift into the world of Atmamun.

I've decided to organize this book with a combination of dialogues and commentary. Many of the dialogues come from conversations I've had with clients.

And I believe in getting straight to the point. I have, thus, kept the chapters short. And I have not kept the reader in suspense. For time is just as precious as the Truth.

What follows is the road to realizing the God that is You.

And the freedom you have searched for for your entire life.

This is the path of Atmamun.

WHAT IS ATMAMUN?

The Sanskrit translation of Atmamun is "Mind of the Spirit."

Imagine if you could train yourself to cultivate the Mind Of the Spirit. What would your life experience be like? How would each day feel? What would you think? How would you see things?

What exactly is the mind of the spirit?

Imagine sitting where you are currently sitting, experiencing everything around you. When I say Experiencing everything around you what I mean is that you are not *thinking* about anything that comes into contact with your five senses.

No matter what sights or sounds you encounter, they do not register as thought, but as experience. You experience them intimately. Without the intermediary known as thought.

As a matter of fact, you have no thoughts whatsoever. You experience everything. You experience it just as it is. Without thinking about it in any way. Just experiencing it. Tasting it. Immersing yourself in it.

Imagine that whatever situation you encounter, your lips

produce the wisest words. You are untouched by anger, or any emotion. You act perfectly. And in perfect proportion to whatever the situation requires.

Imagine that you live in a state of peace. A perpetual high. And that this feeling remains unbroken, no matter the nature or gravity of the circumstance.

Is this not the documented experience of the legendary swamis of the Himalayas?

Is this not what it would be like to be a living God?

This is Atmamun.

You have had moments of complete bliss. Infinitesimal moments in which you felt light, peaceful, and completely joyous. They might have occurred completely independent of the circumstance in which you found yourself. Perhaps while driving along a stretch of highway. Or while cooking dinner. Or even in the midst of a conflict.

Such experiences are often discussed in the setting of athletics. Some have described it as The Zone or a Flow State.

The world refers to this state as resulting from a calm mind. But actually this is not the case.

In such otherworldly experiences, it is not that the mind has been calmed or tamed. It is that, for a small fraction of time, the mind has disappeared!

This is the state of No-Mind.

The Japanese call it *Mushin*. It was referred to in the Tom Cruise movie, **The Last Samurai**.

No-Mind is the gateway to Atmamun.

Atmamun goes beyond the zone and flow states, particularly as they are understood in modern parlance. Atmamun is actually a process that encompasses a deep and nuanced understanding of the human mind.

Atmamun is a process of transcending the mind altogether.

What the mind really is. What gives rise to it. What excites it. What its patterns are. And how it controls our lives.

And *control* is the correct word. All of us are controlled by the mind. Although most people in the world do not realize this. They believe that the decisions that they make are the result of their own conscious logic and reasoning. They believe that their "personality" is an intrinsic part of their fundamental nature. They believe that they are in control of their own lives.

This is an illusion.

Please understand this: **Man's greatest dilemma is that he lives in a prison and he believes that he is free.**

The man who knows that he lives in a prison will find a way to break free of it. But the one who believes that he is free while being imprisoned will remained imprisoned forever.

Through the exploration of the process of Atmamun, he will begin to set himself free. But before he takes his first step upon this journey, he must first realize that he is indeed imprisoned.

In what way is he imprisoned?

In every way possible.

I will explain.

He believes that he likes one thing and dislikes another. Is this true?

No. For it is his mind that likes one thing and dislikes another. You see, the mind cannot live within a state of like or within a state of dislike. It must have both! This is part of the scaffolding upon which it rests. Indeed, the very fact that a preference exists means that mind is doing the "preferring."

The human being is thus imprisoned by his likes and dislikes.

You might ask, *What would I do if I had no likes or dislikes?*

You would take life as it comes. You would experience it. And because you would not be taking sides, you would enjoy it immensely.

Please understand this: **When you have likes and dislikes, you have a desire for one thing and an aversion for another**.

This is a deep and painful imprisonment.

Man goes through life unaware of his imprisonment. That which he considers to be an integral part of life, is actually an integral part of His life. And he does not question this, for all of those around him live similarly.

He is imprisoned by desires, cravings, preferences, prejudices, hopes, wishes, vices, ideals, philosophies, and on and on.

He does not recognize that these are his imprisonment. In fact, he considers them to be a part of his true nature and thus he holds them tight.

The path to Atmamun begins with the recognition that all of these things do not belong to him. They belong squarely to his mind.

And man is Not his mind!

It will perhaps, then, become clear to you that Atmamun is not to improve the mind, but to Transcend it.

Atmamun is not a state of a calm or serene mind. It begins with a state of No-Mind.

This then spawns another question. One that I am constantly asked: *If I transcend the mind, will I not go insane?*

What is ironic is that the mind that is asking this question is itself Insane. I do not intend to be derogatory, or to pass judgment. I mean this quite literally.

We are all Insane!

How so?

For almost every human being in the world, his current existence consists of the following: He has a thought that is generated by his mind. The thought may be true or untrue, logical or illogical, pleasant or unpleasant. This thought produces an emotion within him. It makes him feel a certain way. He then expresses this feeling in the form of a particular reaction or a behavior. That behavior produces a certain tangible consequence.

This consequence then produces another thought. And this thought another emotion. Which leads to another feeling. And another behavior. With another consequence. Leading to another thought.

This is the state of existence for more than 99.9 percent of the population. This is a reactive, robotic, and programmed existence. This sort of existence has the man living as a naked nerve which twitches to every thought, sensation, and circumstance.

This is what I call a Spinal Cord Existence. If you tap the inferior aspect of a person's knee, it produces a kick reflex. Man's entire life is a Kick Reflex.

You might ask, *What is wrong with this?*

Another theme that you will discover throughout this book is that it is not a question of right and wrong. It is a question of misery versus peace. Joy versus anguish. And freedom versus imprisonment.

If we live in this reflexive way, our live will necessarily be filled with pain. For the mind is adept at producing negative thoughts and thus negative feelings and negative behaviors and negative consequences.

The self-help movement has created what it considers to be an antidote for this: *Positive Thinking*.

Positive thoughts still emanate from the same mind. And while they may make one feel more 'positive," it is imprisonment all the same. And you will forever remain lost in the struggle of turning negative thoughts into positive ones.

Bliss is neither positive or negative. Neither is it neutral. It is a state of Equanimity.

You see, any disturbance to a state of equilibrium is a disruption to that equilibrium. Whether the disruption is in an up direction or a down direction matters not. It is a disruption all the same. But in order to circumvent this issue, man has categorized the disruptions as positive versus negative in order to make himself feel better about it.

Nature lives in a state of equilibrium. It does not consider a storm as *bad* and sunshine as *good*. It does not categorize. Or judge. Or take sides.

Nature exists fully and unabashedly according to its fundamental nature.

To understand the fundamental nature of the mind allows one to transcend it. And once the mind is transcended, its powers become available to the human being to use as he pleases.

This is man's fundamental nature.

This is true freedom.

This is Atmamun.

WHAT IS THE MIND?

Before we get subtle, let's begin at the gross level. Let us speak at the wholly practical level. For one can only understand that which is in one's own experience.

The mind is a deeply intricate web. So intricate, in fact, that as you learn more about it you will begin to seriously wonder whether you can distinguish what is mind from what is You.

Inherent in this last statement is the implication that you are not your mind. The mind is not you. But the life that you are experiencing is not being experienced directly by you. It is being experienced by you through the filter of the mind. In fact, this filter is also a projector. The mind creates the entirety of the scene that you experience. Every. Single. Day.

I will illustrate this via dialogue. The questioner will ask questions as Q. and I will respond as KG.

Q: Dr. Gupta, I want to understand what the mind is.

What Is The Mind?

KG: Very well. Let us begin with the form in which you experience it daily.

Q: I'm ready.

KG: Do you have thoughts?

Q: Yes.

KG: These thoughts are mind. Do you have emotions?

Q: Yes.

KG: These emotions come from the thoughts that come from the mind. Do you have irritability?

Q: Yes.

KG: This irritability is mind. Do you feel happiness and sadness and guilt and frustration?

Q: Yes. All of those things.

KG: These all arise from the mind. Do you feel competitive?

Q: Quite often.

KG: This competitiveness is mind. Shall I continue?

Q: So what you are saying is that all of my thoughts and my feelings come from the mind?

KG: Not only that they come from the mind. They ARE mind.

Q: We always hear that the mind is a great thing. That it can move mountains. You seem to be speaking of mind in a negative context. Is mind a good thing or a bad thing?

KG: It is neither good nor bad. These are simply judgments that do not get to the heart of the issue. Let us speak of the issue in terms of what effect it has had on your life, shall we?

Q: Yes.

KG: From the time that you awoke this morning until this evening, how much joy did you experience?

Q: It was just a regular day.

KG: I'm not sure what that means. Are your "regular days" filled with constant joy?

Q: Small moments here and there.

KG: Speaking only of today, how many of those small moments of joy did you experience.

Q: Today? Very few, actually.

KG: And how about yesterday?

Q: Not much.

KG: How about last week?

Q: I see your point.

KG: And what point is that?

Q: That joy is very rare in my life.

KG: Very well. And what is common and frequent in your life?

Q: Basically everything but joy. Joy happens, but very infrequently.

KG: And how many times during the day do you feel a sense of inner quietude or a sense of profound peace?

Q: Almost never.

KG: And how many days in a week do you live free of

even the slightest form of conflict?

Q: Between work and family life, small conflicts happen almost every day. But isn't this normal? Everyone experiences these things.

KG: Absolutely. I'm not singling you out. What you are describing is the life of the vast majority of people in the world.

Q: So what you are saying is that it doesn't have to be this way.

KG: What I am describing is the impact that the mind is having upon your life.

Q: How does the mind do this?

KG: Man is a very adaptable creature. If he lives in prison, he can adapt to the prison. If he lives in misery, he will adapt to the misery. No matter how grave the situation may be, he eventually adapts to it and makes it his home. You and me and the rest of the world have become so enslaved by the mind for so long, that we consider it "normal."

Q: How does all of this happen?

KG: We become enslaved by our minds because we believe that we are the mind.

Q: And this is a problem?

KG: It's the greatest problem in the world. Because as long as you believe that you are the mind, you will become subject to all of the turmoil that the mind is. And the mind is lost in turmoil. The incessant thoughts. The crazy emotions. The wild swings of mood. Jealousy. Anger. Frustration. Envy. Hope.

Desire. Fear. Loneliness. Depression. Anxiety. All of it. For as long as you believe you are the mind, then your life will be filled with these turmoils.

Q: So what is the solution?

KG: Anyone that you go to for help with such problems will attempt to "improve" your condition by attempting to change the mind and alleviate the effect. They will attempt to help you "deal with" the problems created by your mind. But you cannot "deal with" cancer. You must find a way to become completely free of it.

Q: So you don't believe in positive thinking and the other popular therapies that are out there?

KG: Let me ask you a question: Are you bombarded by thoughts all day and every day?

Q: Yes.

KG: Is it not this constant thinking and noise inside your head that is the source of all your anxiety?

Q: Yes, I rarely have a sense of inner quiet.

KG: So what does it matter if those thoughts are positive or negative? They are still thoughts.

Q: But positive thoughts are better than negative ones.

KG: Imagine that you had cancer, and I offered you three choices. One was a medicine that made you vomit four times a week with daily headaches. The other was a medicine that made you vomit twice per week with headaches every other day. And the last was a way to actually break free of the cancer, without

What Is The Mind?

vomiting or headaches. Which would you choose?

Q: The last one.

KG: Positive thinking is the middle choice.

Q: So you are saying that we can break free of our minds?

KG: Yes.

Q: How?

KG: By understanding it.

Q: Can you please explain?

KG: Imagine that you are fighting a war. And that you have found a way to spy on your enemy so that you can see his every move. Wouldn't this allow you to escape him?

Q: Yes.

KG: Imagine that you are sitting in a chair. And I tell you that there is a snake under your chair. Will you need to ask me how fast to get up, or how still to sit, or how to run away?

Q: No. I would just react.

KG: Exactly. You would react in a way that you felt was most appropriate for the situation. And you would do so by your own native intelligence. Once you were given the Insight that there is a snake under your chair, the rest would be relatively easy. The difficulty would arise if you Did Not Know there was a snake under your chair. For then you would become a victim. The difficulty would arise if you did not know when or from where your enemy would strike. For then you would be under his control. Understanding is everything. Understanding is the path to liberation.

Q: So we should view the mind as our enemy?

KG: For the vast majority of us, the mind is indeed our enemy. For it has controlled our lives. The only way to make it a friend, or even a servant, begins with understanding its ways. This is the first step on the path to free ourselves from it.

Q: I understand. Where to we begin?

KG: Let's begin with the mind's most obvious manifestation. The way in which you experience the mind most often. And that is through thought.

Q: Okay.

KG: Have you ever examined your thoughts?

Q: Not really.

KG: Then let's do that now. Think about your thoughts, if you will. What is your thought pattern on any given day?

Q: My mind thinks about a lot of things.

KG: Are those things logical?

Q: Well, if I'm doing a task, it can be logical. But I lose concentration quickly. I often say that I have the attention span of a flea.

KG: You're not alone. And why is this attention span so limited?

Q: Because my mind takes off on tangents.

KG: And are those tangents related to the task at hand?

Q: Usually not. I'll start thinking about the movie I watched yesterday, or even something that happened twenty years ago.

What Is The Mind?

KG: This is the wayward nature of the mind. It flies around the world in a second. It is frenzied. And disjointed. And wild. It is a bird that reacts violently if one tries to cage it. And this is okay. The problem arises when we go with it. And as long as we believe that we are the mind, we will go where it goes. We will run around in a frenzy in lock step with it. We will fly around the world in a second. We will live disjointedly. And we will do everything we can in order to avoid being still. Because movement is the mind's nature, it becomes our nature as well.

Q: So how do we stop it from flying around?

KG: If your dog runs around in the backyard for hours, does it bother you?

Q: No.

KG: What if you were tied to him with a leash? And wherever he ran you had to run as well. Would that bother you?

Q: Yes.

KG: So what would be the solution to this latter problem?

Q: To cut the leash.

KG: Precisely. The dog running around doesn't bother you because you know that you are not the dog. The mind running around does bother you because you are tied to it by a leash.

Q: What's the leash that ties me to the mind?

KG: The belief that you are your mind!

The Path To Atmamun

The mind can go anywhere it wishes. You need not go With It.

The mind can entertain any thoughts that it wishes. They have nothing to do with you.

For you are not the mind.

WHY WORSHIP A GOD?

Millions of people around the world worship and pray to a God.

There seems to be a certain nobility in it. A feeling of goodness. A feeling of belonging to a category of man who is on the right path.

The religious are drunk on the pride of religiousness. And the non-religious man (the discrepant and the heathen, as some call him) has seemingly lost his way. He has succumbed to evil. And lost his sense of morality.

I will tell you something: The pride of religion is more detrimental than the pride of ego. The boastfulness of morality is more sinister than the boastfulness of financial wealth. The high of altruism is no more evolved than the high of substance abuse.

It is a façade created by the man seeking to brand himself under the banner of "morality."

If you placed highly sensitive microphones in prayer halls and religious institutions, what sort of "prayers" would you hear? What sort of "worshipping" would be going on?

In cultures around the world, prayers are not an innocent

homage to the divine. They are a clever transaction. It is bartering at its best. A deal in the "holy" market.

People donate fruit and money to their lord in exchange for a higher pension. Success for their children. A flourishing of their business. To be given a certain gender of child.

It's a black market devoted to the fulfillment of desires. Sanctified by the seal of a manufactured God.

How often are the prayers and the worships about God himself? For his betterment? Without asking for anything in return?

If God does exist, such a one would not be as bad a business man as these people think. Who would give a man a life of riches, in exchange for a coconut? If God does exist, I doubt he pays 50 to 1.

Does God exist?

The answer to this question has no significance to anyone's life. It is a mere curiosity. More senseless concepts upon which to waste our precious existence.

If he exists, your day-to-day existence is still your day-to-day existence. If he doesn't exist, your day-to-day existence is still your day-to-day existence.

Unless you believe the idea that if he existed he would take you in his arms and give you a tour of the heavens. If you do believe this, and this hasn't happened to you, then according to this definition it must necessarily mean that he doesn't exist, does it not?

Why Worship A God?

Understand this: **Man will take any opportunity to avoid that which is most immediate in his life. He will do anything but the task at hand. He will look at anything besides that which stands inches from his face.**

He is an escapist. He is a fantasy-seeker. Illusions are his drug. And reality is of no use to him.

Growing up, I used to read stories of people who claimed that Krishna came and stood before them. Saints who proclaimed that God came and stood before them as real as any man could be. Stories of people who sincerely prayed and upon opening their eyes they saw the God of their worship sitting before them.

Do I believe these stories?

Belief is a useless concept. There is only knowing and not knowing.

Is it possible that people experience such things? Who am I to argue with someone who has claimed such an experience?

Do such things happen? Can they happen? I don't know. This is my honest answer.

What I can say is that I myself have never had such an experience. And thus I must live my life according to the reality that I myself have experienced.

Wherever we wish to go, we can only proceed from where we are. If these stories are a part of your personal experience, then begin from there. If they are not, then begin from there.

If you seek riches, chase them. If you seek fame, cultivate it. If you seek to be a holy man, become one. If you seek success for

Atmamun

your children, help them attain it. If you seek to help the needy, do it.

Do whatever you wish, freely and completely. Without the guilt of morality. Or the burden of should's and shouldn'ts.

Are some of these roads a dead-end? Most certainly. But that does not mean that any man or any God should stop you from exercising your will.

The Path To Atmamun

Do whatever you like. Live in accordance with your sensibilities. Live and work in accordance with your own inspirations.

This is your day-to-day existence. This is Your Life.

What does God have to do with it?

BECOME GOD OR GIVE YOURSELF TO ONE

For the attainment of complete bliss, there are really two ways of dealing with the matter of God. Either way will work beautifully.

If you must believe in a God, imagine for a moment how he lives his life or his existence. Does he experience problems? Does he live in strife? Does he dream about things? Or does he already know that whatever he wants will materialize in front of him? Is he at the mercy of creation? Or is he truly the master of every inch of his life?

Does he live in conflict? Or emotional upheaval? Or at the mercy of the mind? Or do all of these things, nature included, bow at his feet?

There are those for whom the idea of becoming their own God is too intimidating. Or fantastic. Or impractical. They would rather submit themselves to a pre-packaged God.

To submit oneself whole to this God is to achieve bliss. And master life. And become whole. And "enlightened."

Q: I have been a God-fearing woman all of my life. But I have not experienced the bliss that you speak of.

KG: Why do you fear God?

Q: I've always been told to be humble. And to fear God.

KG: I will not ask you the name of your God. For it matters not. Do you see him as one who holds you in the palm of his hand? Or under the weight of his thumb?

Q: I suppose he rewards us and punishes us.

KG: So for you God is like a parent?

Q: Well, I do call him Father.

KG: You already have a father. Why do you need a second?

Q: It is a manner of speech. A sign of respect.

KG: I understand. But in order to reach true bliss, enlightenment, nirvana, or joy in this life, you do not need more authority figures in your life. You do not need "policing." You do not need to live your life hankering for rewards and shunning punishment. This is the way you have lived your entire life. First as a child under the authority of parents. And then as an adult under the authority of God.

Q: I have never in my life heard anyone say that. So what should I do about my God?

Become God Or Give Yourself To One

KG: It is all a matter of sincerity. It is about being crystal clear about what you wish to attain in your life.

Q: I'll tell you what I want. I want this bliss that you always talk about. I'm not sure I even know what it is. But if it means a constant sense of peace or a steady feeling of joy, this is what I want. I'm willing to do anything for it.

KG: I applaud your honesty and your sincerity. Let us then abandon all the games that you've been playing, shall we?

Q: Yes.

KG: I will not take your God from you. But I will begin by asking you what all of the prayers have given you.

Q: A feeling of peace, I suppose. But it's short-lived.

KG: Yes, prayers are the poor man's gold.

Q: How so?

KG: If there is a being who, in your estimation, has the power to give you all that you seek, why would you settle for his good graces? Why would you sit with a begging bowl before him? Wouldn't you want what he has?

Q: Doc, how can I possibly get what God has?

KG: Forget the "how" for a moment. Why would you settle for second or third best?

Q: I don't ever think I would have been bold enough to want what God has.

KG: And yet you are "bold" enough to want uninterrupted bliss in your life?

Q: I haven't been until now. I would love to have what

25

God has. Who wouldn't?

KG: I can perhaps count on one hand the number of people in this world who want what God has.

Q: Why?

KG: Because they consider it "bold" as you do. Perhaps even sacrilegious.

Q: If you're telling me there's a way, I'm ready.

KG: Imagine a leaf that sits motionless on the river bank.

Q: Okay.

KG: As it sits alone on the bank of the river, it has the limited power of a leaf, does it not?

Q: Yes.

KG: If you pick up that leaf and drop it into the raging river, what happens?

Q: The leaf floats along the surface of the river.

KG: Correct. And for as long as it floats along the surface of the river, it moves as the river moves. It sees the various places around the world that the river sees. It breathes as the river breathes. It rolls over ancient stones and leaps across steep cliffs and winds through lush green valleys and ambles through quaint meadows.

Q: Yes.

KG: While a man may look at this leaf and distinguish it from the river that it floats along, does the leaf experience itself as a leaf any longer? Does it still see itself as a limp and motionless leaf with limited power? Or does it now in every way

Become God Or Give Yourself To One

possible assume the power of the river that it has given itself to?

Q: I understand.

KG: The leaf that gives itself whole to the river, Becomes the river.

Q: So what you are saying is that I should give myself to God?

KG: For all of your life, you have held God far from you. You have used him as a wishing well. It matters not who your God is, or where you believe he resides. If you give yourself to him, you will experience your life as he experiences his. You will assume his power. And feel his bliss.

Q: Is there anyone that you know who has done this, Dr. Gupta?

KG: I can think of two beautiful examples. Francis Of Assisi and Meera. These two individuals did not look upon God as a parent. They gave themselves whole to him. And the lives that they lived after having done so were filled with the sort of otherworldly bliss that made the world suspect them as being insane. In a way, they were insane. For they discovered a world which blossomed in front of them in a way that few in the history of civilization ever have. Who wouldn't prefer a life of "insanity" filled with bliss, as opposed to a life of "sanity" filled with turmoil?

Q: Tell me what I need to do, Dr. Gupta.

KG: Imagine that you were boating in a lake. And that you did not know how to swim. Then imagine that the boat

27

capsized and you found yourself submerged in the water. Would you ask me what you needed to do?

Q: No.

KG: What would you do?

Q: I would try to keep my head above water.

KG: Indeed you would. In any and all ways possible. You would flail and kick and pant and do whatever you had to do to keep your head above water. You would not ask for instructions. You would not look for a "how-to" manual or a "self-help" book. You would take matters into your own hands. And you would survive! And the reason that you would survive is because the WHAT would be clearly before you. That WHAT is your life. And because you chose Life, because the What was crystal clear, you would create the HOW for yourself.

Q: You're right.

KG: We must, therefore, establish your What. How clear is this What? How intense is your desire for this What? Does it mean any less to you than surviving from drowning? Is this What a matter of life and death for you?

Q: I've never thought of it that way.

KG: The road to worship and prayer is a crowded road. And it does it not lead to God. The road to the kingdom of God leads directly to him. But this road is deserted.

Q: Why?

KG: Because people are clever. They play ingenious little games with God. They offer a nickel and ask for a fortune. God

Become God Or Give Yourself To One

is simply an insurance policy for them. They have no desire to know him or become him. They seek only to fortify their meager little lives with a few pleasant distractions and a modest sack of wealth and comfort. The kingdom of God is for the rarest man in the world. Millions speak of it. Only One pursues it.

Q: The more you speak the more ashamed I feel.

KG: It is not my intent to make you feel ashamed. It is only my intent to help you establish your What.

Q: My What is complete bliss. To live in joy. But I'm not sure if such a thing is possible.

KG: If you are drowning in a lake, do you weigh possibility and impossibility? Or do you simply act, possibility be damned?

Q: You're right. I simply act.

KG: The human being who is consumed with a particular vision does not allow "possibility" to stand in his or her way.

Q: I'm inspired. I want the kingdom of God.

KG: If you want the kingdom of God more than anything else in your life, you will have it. And the reason that you will have it is because you will not stop until you attain it.

Q: Agreed.

KG: There is no reason to agree. I'm not making a deal with you. In fact, there can no longer be any deals in your life. No compromises. But there will be a cost. And the only question that remains is whether you are willing to pay it.

The Path To Atmamun

If believing in a God is your way, then it let it be your way Completely.

Do not use your God as an insurance policy.

Do not pray to him. Or worship him. Or make requests to him.

Discover what you are using God for.

Discover the ways in which you're playing a clever game.

This requires great Sincerity.

But if you wish to truly attain something or arrive somewhere, this is absolutely essential.

THE PRICE TO ATTAIN GOD

It is a most peculiar thing that, in many cultures, if a boy shows no promise in worldly affairs or if he is deemed to lack talent, he is sent to the priesthood or the ashram.

This is like saying that if a boy has no talent or interest in swimming, he should be sent to the Olympic trials.

The world, in one sense, puts God on a pedestal. And in another sense, it holds him in very low esteem. For it feels that it is the easy path. Or a waste basket institution of sorts for those who have not the dedication or the motivation to succeed in worldly pursuits.

If God is considered by many to be the almighty, then would it not require an almighty individual to pursue his kingdom? Would it not require a man of intense fortitude and single-minded devotion to attain a being that is considered the ruler of the universe?

Any man can join an ashram. Or sit in a church. Or listen to a sermon. Or nod his head in agreement with a motivational guru. But it is a truly rare breed of man who is imbued with the intense motivation to attain even a fraction of what the scriptures teach.

The truth is that holy followers around the world, even the most devoted ones, fail to reach any high attainment in the world of God. They may shave their head. And beg alms. And acquiesce to a life of celibacy. But, in many cases, they are simply part of a group. They enjoy the "idea" of following such a path. The spiritual order is no different than any other worldly institution. There are the common. And there are the elite. And what separates the two is a Sincere and Heartfelt Desire.

Hair is cheap. As is celibacy. As is a comfortable home. As are material goods. Very often, the man who "surrenders" such worldly things feels the ego of having surrendered them. And this become his greatest obstacle to attaining God. He is essentially going through the motions. For somewhere inside himself, even he knows that he got off cheap. He knows that he has not yet paid the ultimate price.

Let us continue the conversation from the previous chapter.

Q: Yes, I am willing to pay the price.
KG: Such things are easily said when the price is not yet known.
Q: You name it.
KG: Very well. If you wish to taste the nectar of life and live in complete bliss, there is no room for You AND God. There is

The Price To Attain God

only room for one.

Q: That's a provocative statement. Can you please discuss this further?

KG: He who chases two rabbits catches neither. He who has one foot in both worlds relinquishes both.

Q: Why must I choose?

KG: Because you and your so-called life are incompatible with the kingdom of God. The way that you have constructed your life allows for God as a consultant and an advisor. As a result, he is always at arm's length. Advice never transformed anyone. The only way that you can attain the kingdom of God is to give yourself whole to the pursuit.

Q: And I can't give myself while living my own life?

KG: To give yourself whole means to have nothing left for yourself, does it not?

Q: But if I give myself whole, how will I be able to experience the bliss in my life?

KG: Imagine that you have spent two weeks lost in the Sahara desert. You are at the edge of death. You are struggling to walk. Your mouth is parched. Your eyes are sunken. And I come to you on a camel, carrying a canteen of water.

Q: Okay.

KG: Now, imagine that I explain to you the chemical formula for water. I explain that water is comprised of two atoms of hydrogen and one atom of oxygen. And that these atoms are joined by covalent bonds.

Q: I'd think you're crazy.

KG: Crazy? Well, what if I explained that water was a colorless fluid. That it could be heated and cooled. And that it flows along a gradient from an area of high concentration to an area of low concentration.

Q: I wouldn't be interested in a science lecture in that circumstance.

KG: What if I told you that it comprised roughly 60% of your body?

Q: It wouldn't do anything for me.

KG: What if I splashed a few drops of water onto your face?

Q: I might feel some relief, but it wouldn't be enough.

KG: Why not? I would have given you a deep knowledge about water. And even allowed you to feel it on your cheeks. What more is there?

Q: I'd want to drink it, of course.

KG: So what you are saying is that you could forfeit the knowledge about the water. But you couldn't forfeit the drinking of it. Is that right?

Q: Absolutely.

KG: Animals large and small know nothing of the chemical nature of water, but drinking it sustains their lives, does it not?

Q: Yes.

KG: My dear friend, is it not the same with God?

Q: I'm not sure I understand.

KG: Knowledge is a cop out. It is a token demonstration of

The Price To Attain God

passing interest. It is a clever little game. For while it may fill the head, it leaves the heart empty. The one and only thing that a thirsty man seeks is to quench his thirst. Unless his thirst is quenched, it is all useless small talk. Is it not?

Q: You're right.

KG: The only way to attain God is to drink him.

Q: And how do I do that?

KG: When I gave you the water in the desert, did you ask me how to drink it?

Q: But that was literal. And this is figurative.

KG: This is because your thirst for God is not yet mature.

Q: Perhaps you're right.

KG: For all of your life, you have been content with the knowledge of God. You have been content with God's chemical formula. Perhaps you have even felt him on your cheeks. But unlike the thirst in the desert, this manner of exposure to him has left you satiated.

Q: Dr. Gupta, please help me understand how I can drink him.

KG: To drink him means to want the kingdom of God more than you want yourself. To drink the kingdom of God means that you are willing to relinquish everything in order to attain it.

Q: What do you mean by relinquish everything?

KG: Fear not. You need not sell your home and retreat into a cave. You need not give away your personal possessions. But in order to make room for him, you must cleanse yourself of the NEED for anything else. All your ideas about life, your attachments to your ideologies, your thoughts about the way things "should be," your preferences, your prejudices. All of it must be on the cutting table.

Q: You really do mean that it's either me or it's him and not both, don't you.

KG: Absolutely. There can be no half way. There is no "partial enlightenment." I asked you to make certain that you were willing to pay the price. The price is your particular understanding of life. The price is all that you consider to be "yours." The price is yourself. And it is non-negotiable!

Q: A hefty price, isn't it?

KG: If you think so, you will never do it.

Q: This is serious stuff.

KG: What did you expect? Do you not realize what you are asking for? You are not asking for a modicum of success, or a better job, or an ounce of riches. You are asking for the Kingdom Of God!

Q: I know I've asked this before, but if I give away myself and all that I know, who will be left to experience the joy?

KG: It is a valid question. We can only know things that we've personally experienced, correct?

Q: Yes.

KG: Until now, whenever you felt joy in your life, you were the Experiencer of the joy.

Q: Yes, I was the experiencer.

KG: When you are the experiencer of the joy, the joy usually

The Price To Attain God

comes from some fortuitous life event. Correct?

Q: Yes, something positive happens.

KG: Precisely. And that positive event is short-lived. Because it is soon followed by a negative event, is it not?

Q: Yes, in my life, negative events seem to outweigh the positive ones.

KG: This is always the case. And even if it weren't the case, it would not make a big difference. For it does not matter how positive the event was, it is short-lived. And thus, the Experience of happiness is also short-lived. And this is how man goes about his life. Hoping for one positive event after another so as to "string together" moments of joy.

Q: I'm with you.

KG: And this will be your fate for as long as you are the Experiencer. For you will sit in wait for the next "positive experience." But if you surrender your life to the kingdom of God, you are no longer sitting in wait.

Q: How so?

KG: Who is it that waits for bliss?

Q: Everyone.

KG: The one who waits for bliss is the one who is not blissful.

Q: So true.

KG: The reason that people are not blissful is because they depend upon Events to make them happy.

Q: Isn't this the way it's supposed to be?

KG: Life is as you make it.

Q: How do I make it otherwise?

KG: The reason that people want joy is because they feel, in a way, miserable. Do you agree?

Q: Misery or unhappiness or disappointment, yes.

KG: And you seek the kingdom of God in order to feel endless joy.

Q: Yes.

KG: And the reason that you crave endless joy is because you feel endless misery.

Q: Yes.

KG: You asked me earlier that if you surrender yourself to the kingdom of God, who will be left to experience the joy.

Q: I did.

KG: My dear friend, if you surrender yourself to the kingdom of God, who will be left to feel the misery?

The Path To Atmamun

Anything of great value has a great price.

If you are asking for no less than God himself, you must give no less than your Entire Self.

YOUR MANUFACTURED SELF

When you look into the mirror, it shows you an image of the person you have habitually come to regard as "yourself."

Because you believe this to be "yourself," you have spent your entire life attempting to adorn him, fortify him, protect him, and guide him.

If someone says anything against this person, you retaliate. If someone tries to harm this person, you rush to protect him. If he is hungry, you feed him. If he is tired, you allow him to rest.

His every little wish is your command. His mundane desires, his need for approval, his hope for success, these are all your life's work. You work incessantly for him. And you never question it. Even the thought of questioning it puzzles you.

It may cause you all sorts of hardship, but you wouldn't have it any other way.

The survival and the well-being of this person in the mirror represents the full sum of your life.

Imagine that I came to you and said that I would take care of this person in the mirror for you. Imagine that I gave you a week's rest. For one full week, I would take care of his needs and attend to all his concerns. From his disappointments about his career to his hope for becoming a success. From his conflict in his family life to his desire for happiness. His hunger, his sleep, his thirst, his sense of peace, you would be free of it all for one week.

What would that week be like?

There would be no worry, for there would be no one to worry about. There would be no hope, as there would be no one to hope for. There would be no boss to impress. Or family member to apologize to.

What would you do with your time? How would you spend the day?

I want you to go there now, within yourself. Fear not, I will not give you the luxury of one week. For man has learned to shun such guilty pleasures. I will only give you a few minutes.

For the next few minutes, this person in the mirror is not your concern. Just for a few minutes. Whether he lives or dies, is tired or hungry, is hopeful or depressed, is not your concern. For the next few minutes, this person in the mirror has no caretaker. His caretaker is taking a break.

Put this book down and do this NOW.

PLEASE DO IT.

Now that you have done so, I will not ask you how you

feel. I will not ask you to tell me what I want to hear. For there is nothing that I want to hear.

Insights are achieved in silence. When they are spoken of, they are poisoned. Feelings are feelings. And, in many ways, to speak is to lie. For language cannot do justice to the subtleties and nuances of feeling.

For your entire life, you have lived as a slave to this person in the mirror. And it has destroyed your life.

This is always the case with slaves. For there is no state that is more lamentable than the loss of one's freedom.

You Are Not YOU

I will briefly outline your life. For your life is the same as every other human being's life. It differs only in the details.

Only the one who seeks Transformation will allow themselves the objectivity to imbibe the following words.

Your life is in turmoil. And you attempt with all your might to Organize the turmoil into a semblance of acceptability.

You beautify the face that you show to others. So that the responses that you receive from them may uplift you.

You raise your children in the image of your own ego. And you often cry in bed at night for the way that you sometimes treat them.

Misery. Hope. Disappointment. Longing. Emotions. These are your bedfellows. And they are at the center of your life experience.

Why?

I will now reveal to you the truth.

The truth that no one has ever before revealed to you.

The life that you are currently living is not your real life. Because you are living through the Sheath known as Mind.

The mind desires, and you believe that it is you who is desiring. The mind craves one success after another. And you believe that it is you who craves. The mind creates your turmoils, and you set off in a frenzy to clean up its messes, believing that it is you who made them.

Your attempt to become a "good person" is an attempt to polish that which is known as ego.

And understand this immediately and clearly: **The Ego is Not that which says that you are great. It is that which says that you Exist at all!**

And now we come to the mind's master stroke. The greatest illusion in the history of man. The sleight of hand that has the entire world enchanted and confused.

The idea that you exist.

This is the one single source of all your problems. This is the genesis of all your turmoils. This is the seed of all your troubles.

Allow me to explain.

Take for instance a lovely woman named, Naomi Johnson.

Your Manufactured Self

Naomi believes that she exists as a person called Naomi Johnson. And thus she will beautify Naomi. She will adorn Naomi. She will have dreams for Naomi. She will have plans for Naomi. She will attempt to make Naomi good and helpful and ambitious and mannerly. She will attempt to make Naomi a success. She will attempt to make Naomi a STAR.

She will spend Naomi's entire life doing these things. And for the entirety of this life, she will live in abject misery.

Why?

Because Naomi Johnson doesn't really exist. The mind that is within Naomi has created this persona that her parents named Naomi Johnson.

And the creation of this persona is the genesis of all of Naomi's problems.

How?

Because whatever happens in Naomi's life does not "just happen." It happens To Her. The breakups, the disappointments, the conflicts, and all of life's endless upheavals happen To Naomi.

As a result, she is simply doomed to a life as a piñata, battered by circumstance. And all the psychotherapy, and meditation, and yoga, and counseling in the world cannot help her.

Why?

Because even as she pursues such remedies, she pursues them As Naomi Johnson.

If you were to shower with your clothes on, would you ever become clean?

The beautiful human beings that I counsel have the world at their feet. They have great wealth and notoriety and all that the material world can offer. Yet what they seek is the Experience of Bliss. And Peace. And Unbridled Freedom.

And this the material world cannot give them.

Here is the Ultimate Truth Of Your Life:

Naomi Johnson is not the person she thinks she is. She is the Being That Knows that a persona called Naomi Johnson has been created.

It is the same for you.

And once you Experience This, the troubles of life may continue in full force. But they will no longer have the power to affect you.

And this, my friend, will be your Doorway to BLISS.

Aren't You Tired Of YOU?

Aren't you tired of looking at yourself? Of the sound of your voice? Of knowing what you are going to say before you say it? Of thinking the same things? Of living with the same opinions?

Aren't you tired of this person that you have lived with your entire life? Aren't you tired of this person called You?

You try to preserve yourself in front of others. But you

Your Manufactured Self

run from yourself in private. You make your opinions known to those around you. And you question them in the quiet of your room.

Is there not a whole new possibility outside of Yourself? Wouldn't you like to be something else? Not someone else. But something else?

Wouldn't you like to see through new eyes? Eyes that see what is actually in front of them. Eyes that seek reality instead of confirmation.

Wouldn't you like to think less? Wouldn't you like to care less?

Wouldn't you like to look into the mirror and see only the mirror? Instead of living Under nature, wouldn't you like it to live through you?

Hasn't this You become a burden yet? For how long will you carry it around? Why not just park it in storage while the non-You goes for a stroll?

Why not leave it to itself while the non-You sees what it has been missing for all these years?

The You that you have been told to look for is the same You that has prevented you from seeing it. Show yourself the non-You. And let those around you see it as well. They will look at you different. They will get lost as they look into your eyes. Because in them they will not see You, but themselves.

They will adore this aimless, opinion-less, transparent You. The non-You.

And the most beautiful thing of all is that it will be evergreen. This non-You will require no maintenance. No care. No adornment.

You will blend into the ether. You will be free of all that has ever concerned you.

Because you will finally be free of the You that brought about all the concerns.

May you never be Yourself again.

Q: I feel peaceful and confused.

KG: That statement is full of promise. What exactly do you mean by it?

Q: I did the exercise and I felt a weight lifted off my shoulders. I literally felt light. But it doesn't make sense. I'm completely confused.

KG: Confusion is a wonderful thing.

Q: Why is confusion a wonderful thing?

KG: When you don't have the answers, a new possibility is on the horizon. When the mind thinks that it knows, it creates a story. And it makes the person believe the fairy tale. But when it is confused, it has no story to tell you. So you are, for a brief moment, free to learn the truth. Independent of the mind.

Q: You just made me more confused.

KG: I'm happy to do so. But tell me about your initial confusion.

Your Manufactured Self

Q: As I said, I felt a huge weight lift off my shoulders when I let the person in the mirror be on her own. But when I thought about it, it made absolutely no sense.

KG: Why not?

Q: Because that person in the mirror is me! How is it even possible that I can 'take a break' from myself? But the funny thing is that that's exactly what I did when I did the exercise. So I actually did it. And it felt wonderful. But when I think about it, it makes no sense why it even worked at all. How can a person leave her own self?

KG: Thought spoils all the fun, doesn't it?

Q: *Laughs.* I guess so. But I have to make sense of it.

KG: This is the problem with us human beings. Receiving something is not enough. Becoming something is not enough. Feeling something is not enough. No matter how grand or majestic that thing may be, we must spoil it with reason. We must graffiti our logic across its sacred presence.

Q: I don't know any other way to be.

KG: I know. It is a habit that you have picked up from the world. And as much as I would like to leave you with the feeling, I know that you will drive yourself mad until you have a proper explanation using logic and reason. So I will indulge you.

Q: Guilty as charged.

KG: You asked how a person can leave her own self. Correct?

Q: Yes.

KG: But for those few moments, that's exactly what you did, isn't it?

Q: I don't really know. All I know is that for those few minutes, I didn't care about this person. And I feel strange calling her 'this person' because I know that that is ME!

KG: But how could it be YOU if you left her?

Q: This is what I don't understand.

KG: Though you may not know it in an intellectual sense, there is something within you that knows that you are not the person you believe yourself to be.

Q: Something inside me?

KG: Yes. Please grab a pen and hold it in your hand.

Q: Okay. I have it.

KG: If I were to ask you what you had in your hand, what would you say?

Q: I would say that I'm holding my pen in my hand.

KG: And when you say 'my pen," what exactly do you mean?

Q: I'm saying that I'm a person who is holding a pen that she holds in her hand.

KG: What you are saying, then, is that there is YOU over here and a pen over there. You are saying that You and the Pen are two different things. This is why you use the designation "my." Correct?

Q: Yes.

KG: Excellent. Now drop the pen.

Q: Done.

KG: What do you have now?

Q: Nothing.

KG: Nothing? What was holding the pen a moment ago?

Q: My hand.

KG: Now, let's discuss that. A moment ago, you said 'my pen." Implying that there was YOU over here and a pen that is Not You over there. Correct?

Q: Yes.

KG: Now you use the phrase 'my hand.' This implies that there is a You over here and a Hand over there.

Q: But I own the hand.

KG: Precisely my point. Someone is owning that hand. And that someone, by virtue of the possessive noun used, cannot be the hand itself. Is this correct?

Q: Yes it is.

KG: So my only question, then, is who is this person that owns the hand?

Q: I'm still confused.

KG: Let me say it in a different way. If I asked you to point to the owner of the pen, where would you point?

Q: I would point to my body. Maybe somewhere toward my chest.

KG: Okay. And if I now ask you to point to the person who owns the hand, where are you going to point?

Q: I'm stumped. I don't know.

KG: This is what I mean by the fact that something within you knows that you are not who you think you are.

Q: So what you are saying is that I am not this body.

KG: What you just said is precisely correct. But this is not the angle I wish to pursue because it relegates the discussion to an intellectual sermon which has little power to change someone's life. It is true that you are Not the body. And that you are Not the mind. But let us proceed with understanding, rather than factual knowledge, shall we?

Q: Yes that sounds good.

KG: Nothing means anything unless it is in one's own experience. Do you agree?

Q: Yes.

KG: I am leading you on a journey away from your manufactured self. And in order to do this, my goal is not to help you escape, but to see. Advisors across the world, be it in the world of psychology or otherwise, are far too interested in treatments and solutions. Treatments and solutions are simply a balm that temporarily soothes the pain. They cure nothing. The only thing that cures is Understanding. The only thing that cures is Clarity. The thing that cures is Not the solution. It is a clear and unflinching examination of the Problem.

Q: I'm with you.

KG: Your problem, by your own admission, is that you lack peace in your life. You don't feel bliss or joy on any consistent basis. Correct?

Q: That's correct.

KG: I will state plainly that the reason for this is because you live as your manufactured self.

Q: Tell me about this manufactured self.

KG: First I will outline it for you. Then we will explore some of the details in greater depth.

Q: Sounds good.

KG: When you look in the mirror, you see a body and a face. You have completely and totally accepted this body and this face as You. You choose to dress this body in a certain way. Groom yourself in a certain way. Part your hair in a certain way. You have opinions about many things. Opinions about politics, society, abortion, finances, hard work, raising children, education, diet, philosophy, religion. You decide to walk a certain way. You decide to carry yourself in a certain way. All of these things are strategically designed to portray the image that you have of yourself. This is what you call Your Personality. All of this is what you call You. And it is what I call the Manufactured Self.

Q: By saying that it is manufactured, do you mean that it is false?

KG: You ask a wonderful question. Naturally, if something is manufactured, it is not in its original state. But I don't wish to be derogatory or condemning. I want us to walk together on this journey toward an organic understanding.

Q: Okay.

KG: The problem with manufacturing anything is that it requires continuous maintenance. It requires constant support. It needs to be looked after and checked upon and groomed and trimmed. And in this way it very much becomes a burden. My backyard consists of patches of lawn bordered by a fence. And behind the fence is a natural wooded area. The patches of lawn must be constantly and intensely maintained. They must be watered with sprinkler systems and cut with mowers and fertilized and trimmed. The wooded area needs no maintenance. The rains water it. The animals play within it. The wind caresses it. Nature assumes its care. And it is just as beautiful as the carefully manicured lawn. Without any need of maintenance.

Q: That makes perfect sense. But it's almost like you're saying that we should not take care of ourselves.

KG: What I'm saying is that because you have manufactured a self, you have to constantly look after it.

Q: How is my manufactured self not my real self?

KG: The vast majority of your ideas, opinions, likes, dislikes, and philosophies were not ones that you were born with. You acquired them like pieces of clothing. They became the scaffolding for this manufactured self. And each day that you awake, you have to jump into the skin of the manufactured self. It is a role that you play.

Q: How so?

KG: If someone says something against this self, you feel a powerful need to protect it. If it does not get what it desires, you feel disappointment. If it loses something, you feel sad. If it gains something, you feel happy. And as I'm saying these things, you think that this is normal. And the reason that you think this is normal is because everyone around you also does the same thing. For normalcy is nothing more than a democratic madness.

Q: So what should I do?

KG: You ask this question too easily and too quickly, dear friend. I will not allow you to flee from the full weight of the truth through an escape chute. You don't seem to understand how much of a burden this personality, this manufactured self, has become to you.

Q: I've felt burdened quite often.

KG: You felt burdened by the weight of some responsibility. But I'm speaking of the burden of having to maintain and tend for this manufactured self.

Q: How does it burden me?

KG: Because you constantly seek to satisfy its every wish, you live in constant anticipation. Because you seek to wipe away its sorrows, you seek desperately for its happiness. Because you seek to maintain its reputation, you are acutely sensitive to the sharp opinions of others. Everything that you do is done in the interest of its welfare. It has made you a slave.

Q: So this manufactured self is responsible for all of my unhappiness?

KG: Who is the person who seeks to be happy? The person that you call You. And who is this You? Your manufactured self.

53

Do you not see? Even the need for happiness is a great burden. You would not have this need if you had no manufactured self.

Q: So what you are saying is the very persona that I'm using to Overcome my problems is actually the Cause of my problems.

KG: That is correct. When the manufactured self is created, problems are as well. The manufactured self is nothing more than one gigantic problem. And man lives his entire life trying to untangle a mess, when all he needs to do is to step out of it. When YOU are born, misery is born. When YOU are born, burden is born.

Q: That would be easy to take the wrong way, wouldn't it?

KG: No question about it. Because most would feel that I'm attacking something about their personality. But what I'm attacking is the very idea of Having a personality.

We are slaves to ourselves. And we think that we are free. The greatest freedom that we have is the freedom to walk away from ourselves.

I will say this again: **The greatest freedom that we have is the freedom to walk away from ourselves.**

The day that you walk away from yourself, you no longer feel the need for happiness. For bliss has become yours.

Why?

Because there is no longer any burden to carry. There is no great master to take care of. You are absolved of your responsibilities. You are now officially off duty.

You are free to dance in the fields. And roam in the hills.

In becoming nothing, you have gained everything.

The Path To Atmamun

The single greatest obstacle to Atmamun is the presence of your manufactured self.

The person that you call "myself" is the source of all your miseries.

Remove this manufactured self, and you will be as free as a living God.

IS YOUR LIFE REALLY A LIFE?
. . . REALLY?

You spend your life chasing Things.

You chase after success. You hope for riches. You strive for respect. You value accomplishment.

Why?

Because you have no choice.

The hole within us is so big, the chasm so wide, the emptiness so unbearable, that we must fill it with something.

Nature abhors a vacuum?

No sir. Nature nurtures a vacuum. It is man that abhors it.

The man who cannot stand being a Nobody will strive to become a Somebody. But as he chases this status, he finds that this Somebody he hopes to create never seems to sustain itself.

Therefore, he must keep creating and re-creating this person. But try as he might, he can never make flesh and bone out of it. It remains forever a shadow on the surface of the water.

And if he looks back at his life, he wonders what it all amounts to? What do his accomplishments really mean? What have they done for him besides afford him a certain level of comfort and a smattering of applause?

To be the best in the world at one's craft is largely a journey into the recesses of one's self, rather than a journey toward a stage. To arrive at one's goal broken and battered and soul-less, no matter how grand the achievement, is to have arrived nowhere.

As it is put so beautifully in the bible, What good does it do a man to gain the world and lose his soul?

A man's greatest prize is his own Life. Not the life he creates. Not the life he hopes for. Not the life he manufactures. Not the life he adorns. Not the life he strives for.

But the life he was born with. That deep, nameless, pulsating vibration that spawns breath in his lungs and consciousness within his being.

The life that existed before the life he attempted to create.

Imagine for a moment what it would feel like to Want For Nothing! To live your days invested completely in that which you love to do. Your art, your passion . . .

But Without A Single Iota Of Hope.

To live your life as someone who had no need to attain anything else for the remainder of his life. Whatever comes, let it come. And whatever does not, isn't even noticed. For it was never Hoped For in the first place.

Understand this: **Hope Destroys!**

If who you are today is not enough, it is because you don't know who you truly are. And trying to make yourself into Someone will take you even further away from who you fundamentally are.

To live a Hope-less life is simply the most glorious life of all.

To live as nothing. To hope for nothing. To strive for nothing.

The man who lives in this way gains accolades without wanting them. And he becomes a Prince of Mankind.

I ask you: Is it not forever better to live as a Prince, rather than as a Pauper?

Life Is Not What You Believe It To Be

Do you recall the shape of a sine wave?

It is composed of peaks and troughs that recur at regular intervals.

A sine wave is a perfect mathematical representation of the life of the average human being.

Because the average human being lives his life according to Events, he suffers both the rises and the falls. The happiness and the turmoil.

And do not make the mistake of believing that happiness and turmoil, and pain and pleasure are opposites. For I assure you they are not. They are very much two sides of the same coin.

If you are happy, don't get too excited, for misery is just around the corner.

Is Your Life Really A Life? ... Really?

And if you are unhappy, fear not, for happiness is on its way.

This is the purgatory of man. To live vacillating between opposite poles of emotion. Living in This whilst hoping for That. Loving This whilst hating That. Striving for This whilst receiving That.

Must it be this way?

Yes!

Why?

Because the events of the world are precisely this. It can be no other way. Some events will be in your favor. While others will be to your detriment. And you will continue to suffer the friction of both.

Is there a way out?

There is a way out. But only for a very specific sort of human being.

The human being who sees the sine wave for what it is. And cares for it no more! The human being who sees the strings behind the stage. The human being who understands that the events of his life will bring him nothing of any real value, or any lasting bliss.

When this sort of human being encounters something auspicious, he will likely feel a surge of excitement. But he will immediately recognize that it is from the mind. And thus his excitement will abate.

When he encounters something troubling, he will feel his heart drop. But he will immediately recognize that this too is from the mind. And his disappointment will simply vanish.

What this human being will begin to understand is that Life has nothing to offer him. That nature has structured life in such a way that bliss is only available in the most mundane of places: This Very Moment. And nowhere else!

That which appears exciting is a charade. That which appears disastrous is as well.

We live in a world of shadows and mirages. Nothing is real. Nothing is tangible. Nothing belongs to You. Nothing is under your control.

Life is something that is to be Lived rather than manufactured.

But the Living can only happen if we live as a lonely traveler passing through. Rather than one who builds his home and settles down within it.

You can build your home if you like. But understand that you are building it on shifting sand. And, as such, it will one day crumble. And your so-called life will come crashing down.

Live your life as a lonely stranger. As a wanderer filled with awe and wonder.
Leave everything as you found it. For none of it belongs to you.

Let the events happen around you, knowing that none of them are happening TO You. And you will live an equanimous life.

You will live a life without the burden of hope. Or the weight of despair.

In doing this you will have known life for what it is. And what it is not.

And wisdom and equanimity will finally be yours.

Make Your Life A Benediction

If I told you that this world was a hall of mirrors, you wouldn't believe me.

Nor should you. For a man should not allow "belief" to be his guide, lest he lose himself in the darkness.

It is important to look at the results. It is important to look at the state of things. It is important to look at the way things are.

And ask yourself if you are satisfied with them.

One of the most useful qualities of human beings is also their poison. And this is the quality of Adaptability.

As history has shown time and again, a human being can adapt to any circumstance and any condition. And while this may afford him a mode of survival, it rarely affords him a mode of Life.

If a man suffers, he becomes accustomed to the suffering. Suffering becomes his companion. And thus he spends the whole of his life looking for minor nuggets of joy within this ocean of suffering.

The reason that human beings do not live a life of bliss is because this is not what they hold most dear. Their eyes are fixed upon the twinkles on the horizon. Their hearts are fixed upon the drug of achievement. Their attention is fixed upon the search for happiness.

They recognize that such things are fleeting. And thus they feel that they must have them in bulk.

What they cannot create in quality, they must make up for in volume.

They are hooked by the occasional reward. And this keeps them bound to the world.

If my ancient brethren of the Himalayan snows discovered anything it was that the world had nothing to offer them. Experience had taught them that living in the world was akin to walking in a big circle, chasing shadow after shadow.

There is a wonderful story of a young professional who went to see a Himalayan swami.

Swamiji, he said, "I admire your courage. For what a sacrifice you have made. To live as a renunciate. To have given up the entire world and live in a cave."

The swami laughed, and said, "My dear boy. I once lived in the world. And I discovered that in chasing this and that, I lived in constant anxiety and misery. Now I live in complete bliss. My every moment is an overwhelming joy. You have chosen the world and its miseries, and have given up joy and bliss. Tell me, young man. Is it I who is the renunciate? Or you?"

Lest you become afraid, I am not asking you to retreat into a Himalayan cave.

Is Your Life Really A Life? . . . Really?

In fact, I'm not asking you to do anything. For this is not my way.

I will only ask you this: Is what you have renounced worth that which you continue to chase?

Is the life that you live a life of Adaptation? Or a life of ceaseless joy?

If there is one truth that I have learned, it is that unless you find it inside of Today, you will never find it inside of Tomorrow.

Your life will become a benediction the day that you stop searching. For as long as you continue to search, you will keep sacrificing Today.

For as long as you continue to search, you will be bound to the idea that there is something to find.

For as long as you continue to search, you will become in love with the search.

The Bible says, Seek and ye shall find.

But perhaps the seeking it is speaking of is not the seeking in the world. But a seeking within yourself.

You see, once you seek inside, you no longer have the need to find. The search will be over.

A man who pursues his passions and experiences his life with complete boldness has no need to search.

He simply lives.

He walks toward no horizon. For he has already seen beyond it.

This, my friend, is the benediction.
To abandon the world.
And gain the universe.

The Path To Atmamun

Life does not happen around you. It is not a chronology of events.//
Perceiving life in this way keeps you on the edge of life.
Ask yourself: What does it mean to LIVE?
And you will discover that you've never really LIVED at all.
Life is to be tasted.
Drink it.
Immerse yourself in it.
And experience it for the very first time.

LIFE IS THE ULTIMATE ABSURDITY

What is the meaning of life?

This is on the lips of millions of human beings. And every one of these human beings is an adult.

Have you ever heard a child ask this question?

The one who asks the question is the one who has not tasted life. The one who asks this question is the one who looks at life as a means to a particular end. For *meaning* is an intellectual concept. Intellect affords a sense of survival in the modern world. But survival is survival. And living is living.

The child who twirls in the rain has no purpose for doing it. The child who runs through the field does not run to get somewhere. The running and the jumping and the playing is not done for *meaning* or *purpose*. It is an expression of the elation within. It is not done For joy. It is done Out Of joy.

You can try to organize your life into neat and organized sections. You can label it and categorize it. You can arrange it in any way you wish. But the minute you turn your head, it will become amorphous once again. You cannot contain it any more than you can contain the ocean.

A mountain breeze has no meaning. A floating cloud has no meaning. A surge of emotion has no meaning. A glorious idea has no meaning. Successes. Accolades. Achievements. Feelings. None of these things have meaning.

Certainly, man will ascribe meaning to them. Man will slice it this way and that and look at it from all angles in order to Reduce It into a meaning. But this is only because man is not interested in what IS. He is only interested in what he can Make Out Of It.

And this is why the bulk of humanity lives a Clinical existence. It reeks of antiseptic and medicines, rather than undefined aromas.

You can create anything you wish In your life. But you will never make anything Out Of life. For life will always be life. Meaningless. Innocent. And Indefinable.

Some will read my words and assume that I am condemning the pursuit of success or the procurement of wealth. I would argue that my words are, in fact, providing even more freedom to do so.

You see, if your pursuits and exploits in life have meaning to you, you will be burdened by expectation. You will feel the weight of striving. You will feel the pain of hope. You will be exposed to turmoil and disappointment and hardship along the entire journey.

Buddhist monks spends weeks creating an intricately patterned mandala with painstaking detail. Millions of grains of sand are required. And an unwavering focus to exact every detail. And when it is complete is a beautiful work of art.

What do the monks do after the mandala is complete? Do they cherish it? Do they put it into a frame? Or save it as a gallery piece with the other mandalas?

No. They destroy it.

This is their way of teaching themselves impermanence. And as strange as it may sound, there is joy in freeing oneself from the attachment to his own creation. For attachment is the greatest bondage in existence.

Climb the greatest mountain. Achieve all the accolades in the world. Become the greatest in your field. Achieve fame. Earn millions.

And you will enjoy every bit of the journey, if and only if you understand that none of it means anything.

When something has meaning, it becomes work. When something is meaningless, it becomes play. The joy that you experience in honing your craft is the greatest reward. Spending your life exactly the way you wish to spend it is a wonderful liberation. This is what sinks into the heart. This is the true experience. And understand this: life's nectar lies in experience, rather than reward. Rewards fade from memory. Experiences remain forever.

A life of wild abandon is the greatest life. Leave purpose to the wind. Give yourself to your life. Surrender yourself to your inspirations. Achieve all the greatness in the world. And be

willing to drop it without hesitation.
>This is a life of joy.
>This is a life of freedom.

Life Is Not A Wishing Well

The biggest problem that we as human beings face is not understanding life. We build our homes on fault lines and we suffer the inevitable earthquakes that result.

Life is a wild beast. It is as it is. For all human beings.

At once, ugly and beautiful. It has never been tamed. It will never be tamed.

The messages that surround us say that we deserve happiness. That life is good. That life will give us what we ask if we are willing to work for it.

My friend, life will not give you anything.

Not because it is evil or cruel. But because it has not the capacity to give. It is simply there.

>It can be experienced. It can be drank. It can be explored.
>But it is not a wishing well.

It is simply there to do with as you please.

It is a tempest that we all travel through. The problems arise when we think of it as our friend. Or when we believe that it should be gentle.

>Life is as raw as all forces of nature. And what we perhaps

must realize is that our suffering comes from expecting it to be that which it can never be.

Each moment breathed is a moment lived. To experience life in every breath. Just as it is.

Knowing this, perhaps we can move forward.

Life Is Not What You Think

Life . . .

We attempt to make meaning out of it. We attempt to shape it into significance.

We attempt to adorn it with ideals. We attempt to look into it and find ourselves.

We are all such fools. Yet we think we are wonderfully intelligent. We marvel at our cleverness. We believe we understand life.

We do not.

Life has never had any meaning. The meaning that one finds in life is the meaning he ascribes to it.

Life is simply a joke. An absurdity. A non-linear, haphazard, and unpredictable trail that is fertile for the imagination of hallucinatory human beings.

Life is a Rorschach. You can see in it what you wish.

It is a mirage. Always tempting us to see some glimmering landscape on the horizon.

If you deconstruct life, and break apart all of the pieces

and look at it, bit by bit, you realize that it is not what you thought it was. Instead of pages of prophecy and significance and biography, you find the intelligible gibberish of an infant tapping on the keys of a typewriter.

You've been chasing a ghost, my friend. When things were going well, life had no intention of treating you right. And when things were sour it had no intention of treating you ill. The events that surround us just surround us.

There is no grand plan. And there never was one.

There is just an open field upon which to play.

By all means, build your house. But understand that it will be a house of cards.

By all means, make your mark. But understand that someone will one day erase it.

By all means, change the world. But understand that after you die, it will change back.

I am not a pessimist. Nor am I an optimist.

I am a seeker. My way is the way of truth. In any form in which I can find it. I will tell you firmly that that which I know pales in comparison to that which I do not.

But this much I know: **Life is not what you think it is**.

What is life?

Life is the leaf that falls and tumbles onto a bed of leaves.

Life is the dog that barks in the distance.

Life is a breeze which blows through your hair.

Life is the very thing that you ignore every day.

Life Is The Ultimate Absurdity

Life is the most insignificant event of the hour.

Life is not a series of events. Rather it is the substrate in which the events take place.

We have a habit of looking at life in a certain way. We have a habit of looking at it in a good or bad light depending upon the nature of the events that we experience. But events do not color life any more than smoke colors the sky.

Perhaps the greatest realization we can have is that we are free to do whatever we wish. But in order to remain in this freedom, we must discard the notion of significance.

My friend, there was a day that you were not here. And there will soon be a day when you are no longer here. And once you realize this, you will understand that all there is left to do is play.

Play with your work. Play with your kids. Play with your wife. Play with your surroundings. Play with your happiness. Play with your sorrows. Play with all of those things that you consider to be your miseries and misfortunes.

There is no linear path. There is no destination on the horizon. If you wish to create one, play with that as well.

If you attempt to Make A Life, you will miss it.

If you attempt to Create Significance, you will lose your freedom.

And if you lose your freedom, what life is there left to live?

The Path To Atmamun

To intellectualize life is to miss it completely.

If you understand that life has no meaning, the events of your life will not affect you.

You will move through the world with ease.

For you will have acquired the wisdom to live life as a poetry, rather than a stale and confining prose.

WHY YOUR LIFE IS FILLED WITH PAIN

What I am about to tell you is what the world never will.

It is what your parents never have, for they were not in a position to do so.

It is what your churches, and your temples, and your priests, and the motivational speakers, and the psychologists have never ever told you.

You have forever been on the road to pain. And you are headed toward more pain.

And it is precisely this understanding that will lead to bliss. It is precisely this understanding that will finally lead to your freedom.

If you believe that water can be extracted from a stone, you will spend your entire life chiseling away at that stone. But if you do so, you will have wasted your life. For the stone cannot give you what it does not have.

You believe that your life is supposed to be filled with joy. And with satisfaction. And with peace. And with freedom.

And because you believe this, you look here and there. You enter into this relationship and that relationship. You move from one city to another. You transfer from one job to the next.

You try meditation. You speak to priests. And go to the church. And read self-help books. And watch motivational speeches.

And although you very occasionally taste a drop of joy, it soon retreats into a familiar feeling of disappointment and anxiety.

Why?

Because you have never been told the truth. And even if by some chance you were, you never truly understood it.

The life that you are currently living is a life of Events. One after another.

A job interview. A chance meeting. A bridal shower. A run-in with a store clerk. An upcoming deadline. An encounter with your son or daughter. A promotion. And so on.

Such are the events that surround you. Such are the events that give you anxiety and happiness and disappointment and fear and stress and hope . . .

If the event does not go in your favor, it will lead to pain Immediately. If the event goes in your favor, it will lead to pain Tomorrow.

Why the latter?

Because you live Within this construct known as your Mind, you look at things through The Mind's Eye. And since the mind, by its very nature, cannot be satisfied, achievement only leads to the Need for more achievement.

Why Your Life Is Filled With Pain

Money leads to the need for more money. Sorrow leads to the need for more happiness. And happiness leads to the need for even more happiness.

In such an existence there is no such thing as contentment. For contentment is mind's kryptonite.

The Mind lives for Tomorrow. For it simply cannot live today.

Your entire life, no matter how deep and significant you may think it to be, is essentially a frenzied rush toward Peace.

But you will Never find peace.

Never!

Why?

Because for as long as you believe that This Life Of Yours will give you peace, you will continue to search for peace in the events that you encounter. But those events are fleeting. And thus your sense of peace is as well.

The only human being that discovers lasting peace is the one who finally sees through the game. The one who finally understands what lies behind the curtain. The one who pieces together the bits and pieces of this puzzle of past life events.

And when he sincerely does, he or she begins to laugh. For he sees that he has been attempting to extract water from a stone.

My dear friend, this life can offer you nothing but pain. You have lived in pain and misery for all your life. Most people do not even realize this. And thus they live imprisoned forever.

But this is your only chance at freedom. For when you see that life is inherently and fundamentally full of strife, pain, disappointment, anxiety, and misery, you will stop looking for bliss within the events of your life.

You will stop attempting to "replace" negative thoughts with "positive" ones. You will stop attempting to "reframe" the pain into something more psychologically palatable.

And when this understanding seeps into your bones, you will see "your life" for what it is.

And you will perhaps for the first time in your life begin to actually Live.

You will begin to live inside this very moment. Not because of silly little prescriptions such as "mindfulness" but because you fundamentally will have understood that to live anywhere else is simply a lie.

Why would you go anywhere else if you no longer believed that that "somewhere else" had nothing to give you?

You will Experience your children. You will Experience the slight bend in the road. And the gentle slope of the mountain. And the wayward twirl of the leaf as it falls onto the surface of wet stones.

Your life will become a benediction. And you will have discovered the life that nature has always lived.

And the one that it has always intended for you to live.

The Path To Atmamun

Prescriptions such as positivity, mindfulness, optimism, and happiness are traps.

They will keep you invested in an activity, an undertaking, a "doing" of some sort.

If you try to be mindful, you will never leave the mind.

If you chase after happiness, you will attract unhappiness.

If you convert negative thoughts into positive ones, you will be converting for the rest of your life.

Peace is not known Eventually.

It must be had Now!

No prescriptions. No tricks. No potions. No techniques.

Simply Understanding.

Simply seeing the game you've been playing for your entire life.

This and this alone will lead you where you have always wanted to go.

HUMAN BEINGS WERE NOT MEANT TO BE WORKERS

There is a famous story of a lion cub who lost his way and found a group of sheep. As he lived with the sheep, he became a sheep. He began to walk like one and make sounds like one. Until one day a lion noticed this strange sight and he asked the cub what he was doing. The cub explained that he was a sheep. The lion took him to a nearby lake and asked him to look at his reflection. The cub suddenly realized that he was a lion. And upon realizing this, he began to roar.

In this world, there is an enormous value placed upon getting a "job." Men toil in labor in exchange for a "paycheck." This is considered to be an honorable way to live. And it is considered honorable because it is compared against the individual who is given to sloth, and a dependence upon government assistance or handouts for his existence.

It is true that the man who is given to sloth and dependency is deplorable. But it is also true that the man who toils in exchange for a paycheck is a slave. Some will consider my words harsh. Some will consider it an affront against the working class. It is important to understand that I am also guilty of this affront against my own humanity. And I am on the mend.

A "job" is an insult to a human being. For a human being is a prince of men. He is a king of existence.

We have lost our way. And have taken comfort in the company of sheep. And the time has come for us to look at our own reflection.

The man who is in love with his trade is not a worker. He is an artist. Whether he makes a million dollars or a thousand, he is living in accordance with his nature. And thus his days are filled with joy.

The man who works "for a living" and who is not interested in what he does, is a laborer. It matters not if he has a corner office, four secretaries, and a five million dollar salary. He is insulting the glory of his own creation.

You may tell me your sentimental story of the family that you must support and the children that you must feed. But it will fall on deaf ears. For the greatest nourishment that you can give your children is an inspirational role model who sets the stage for their own future.

Food is overrated. Man is hungry for inspiration. Man is hungry for inner abundance. Man is hungry for the realization of his true potential.

Man is hungry to retain the right of his kingship.

Your "job" may indeed earn you a living, but it will not earn you a life. It may put food on your table, but it will not nourish you. It may provide you with drink, but it will

not quench your thirst.

It will simply allow you to survive. And, my dear friend, you were meant for so much more than that.

I will tell you to do precisely what the religions and the holy men forbid. I will tell you to achieve. I will tell you to find your talents. I will tell you to explore your abilities. I will tell you to make a name for yourself. I will tell you to make millions. I will tell you to live in luxury.

Because you are a King!

Some will say that rich people are unhappy. And that a successful person is not always content. I do not discount the validity of this claim.

In response to this I will say that I am not advocating a life of success or riches. I am not saying that one should seek these things. Nor am I saying that one should not seek these things. You see, it seems to be a trend in the world of spirituality to discount a life of comfort and settle for a life of poverty. There is a long tradition in spirituality to demonize wealth.

I believe that this philosophy is misguided. And the reason that I believe this is because it speaks only a partial truth. Money is Not the root of all evil. Firstly, it has nothing to do with good versus evil. For it is not a question of good or evil. It is a question of joy and misery.

There are just as many miserable people on the spiritual path as there are on the worldly path. If we are going to discuss wealth and success and its relation to bliss, let us use the honest truth, rather than judgment and condemnation.

What is the unbiased honest truth?

The unbiased honest truth is this: Wealth, success, and luxury do not harm a man. What harms a man is the Attachment to these things.

If a man becomes greatly successful and accumulates a treasure chest full of wealth, he is not the worst for it. But if he is attached to these things, he is doomed.

And what is rarely mentioned is also this: The man who is Attached to the idea of achieving spirituality is equally doomed.

Attachment is poison. Attachment is the source of all misery. Attachment to money, fame, ego, success, spirituality. Even attachment to family and friends.

Attachment is the antithesis of life. Attachment is the great death. A death greater than death itself.

Man is a king. But he believes that he is a beggar who must work toward becoming a king. And because he believes this, he lives his entire life as a beggar.

The king is not the one who possesses wealth. The king is the one who is whilst possessing it, remains unattached to it. Because he does not feel an intimate ownership of it, he is not owned by it.

A king is not a king Because of his riches. A king is a king Despite his riches.

Therefore, when a man takes pride in being a worker or for having a "job" for the purpose of receiving a paycheck, he is a beggar. He may earn a six figure salary. But he remains a beggar.

Many will protest this statement. They will say that it is honorable to provide for one's family. They will say that having a job in order to support the family is a source of pride and responsibility.

To this I will respond in the following way. Every man in this world has a talent. And the vast majority of them have been taught to ignore it.

Is there "pride" in this? Does this show a "responsibility" toward one's own Self?

On the airplane, we are told to secure our oxygen masks before we help another with their oxygen mask. This is beautifully symbolic. For the world teaches us exactly the opposite. And it is for this reason that man suffocates in a world filled with oxygen.

Unless a man first helps himself, he cannot really help another. As Shakespeare said, To Thine Own Self Be True. Unless you are true to yourself, you cannot possibly be true to another. Unless you first help yourself, you cannot possibly help another.

I receive many telephone calls and emails from people who ask me how to become a success. They tell me that they are tired of their job. They say that they wish to do work which fulfills them but they don't know where to begin.

I have written about this often. And I will say that when a

Human Beings Were Not Meant To Be Workers

man asks me such a question, he is being disingenuous with me, and dishonest with himself. If I set your house on fire, you would not sit amidst the inferno and ask me what to do. You would surrender to your instincts and do anything and everything to save yourself.

The person who asks me How to do something is not serious. He is simply looking for solace. He is looking for someone to sympathize with his plight. He is looking for someone to tell him that it is Okay that he did not spend his life exploring and discovering the talents that nature bestowed upon him.

If I gave this man advice on How to become a success, I would become an accomplice. And in becoming an accomplice, I would serve to keep him exactly where he is. For each "answer" that I would give him would only embolden him to ask more questions. And he would ask and ask and ask, all the while remaining exactly where he is. This is, in fact, his clever game. To ask as many questions and How's as possible so as to free himself from the guilt of doing nothing, and grant himself the luxury of staying exactly where he is.

I will not help a man remain a beggar. I will applaud him when he recognizes that he is one. And I will embrace him when he sincerely decides to walk toward his own Kingship.

Once this decision is made, together we will create a path for him. A journey toward that which is rightfully his. But only once he sincerely decides. And not one moment sooner!

I do not condemn a man for having a job. I chastise him for believing that this is all he is worth. I call him out for his unwillingness to examine his interiority and discover that he is a Prince of the earthly kingdom.

There are glorious talents that are unique only to You. For nature does not make carbon copies. And schools and societies insist upon nothing but carbon copies.

One day you will die. And when you are in your final days, how you will you feel when you realize that you spent your life as a "worker?" How will you feel when you realize that you have wasted your entire life never having explored the talents that were meant only for You? How will you feel when you discover that you have left your riches on the table? How will you feel when you realize that you sold yourself for a shilling?

You are fortunate. For there is still time.

What will you do with it?

The Path To Atmamun

Nature created you as an original.

Originals are invested with glorious talents.

Discover the talent within yourself that nature has been waiting for you to show to the world.

Human Beings Were Not Meant To Be Workers

You are a creator. And you always have been.

Give yourself the permission to create.

For if you do not, the world will take advantage of you being ignorant to this fact. And it will put you to "work!"

BECOME A LEGEND IN YOUR FIELD

Man is addicted to mediocrity. It is in the water that he drinks. And in the words that he hears. It is in the faces of those around him. And on the lips of those who surround him.

He is taught to get a "job." And to "improve." And to "make a living." And to "survive."

These sentiments are representative of living at the lowest rung on the ladder of human possibility. They are a scraping of the bottom of the barrel of human existence.

It is so incredibly difficult to think of yourself as a legend, isn't it? The mind doesn't easily give in to this idea. It fights it every step of the way. But it doesn't need to fight much. For few ever entertain this idea about themselves. And most of those who do, end up dropping it altogether.

If you look at any industry you will see that they all do things the same way. If you look at any profession you will notice that they all get similar results. All of them follow each other. And while following each other, they hope to differentiate themselves from one another. Is this not a direct contradiction?

Let us look at the world of professional sports. What is

the one thing that is common to almost all sports?

Parity.

Each player is attempting to outdo the other by just the slightest margin. Thousands of a second, a single point, a single goal, a single shot. And they devote their lives to the possibility of victory by infinitesimal margins. It is the same with the corporate world.

Let us look at professional golf as an example. The PGA Tour is the grandest stage in professional golf. Players on the PGA Tour have markedly different strengths, physiques, and talents. Some are super long drivers of the ball. Others have great short games. A few have both. Some are great putters. Some cannot putt. Some are strong. Some are not. Some have years of experience. Others are rookies. Some possess a certain mental fortitude. Others cave under pressure. The players differ significantly in their physical attributes, years of experience, skill levels, mental capacity, perception, degree of determination, physical power, and so on.

And despite the multitude of differences, time and time again the margin of victory on the PGA Tour is A Single Stroke!

How is such a thing possible?

The fact that few even ask such a question is further evidence of man's adaptability. No matter how outrageous a result or situation is, if he is exposed to it enough times, he accepts it as the norm. He Adapts to it and files it in his brain as "normal."

When I was first exposed to golf, this among other things were so glaring that they slapped me in the face. But the bigger slap in the face came from noticing that no one else seemed to question, or even notice such things. As an outsider, there were bells and sirens going off in my mind. But to the insider, all was "normal" and status quo.

It wasn't until years later when I began working with players on the PGA Tour that it became more clear as to why this was the case. The concept of adaptability was the greatest factor. But when I stood inside the ropes watching the manner in which professional golfers trained and how they lived and functioned in this environment, the puzzle was solved.

It became clear to me that the tour players were not differentiating themselves from each other. In fact, they were growing Toward one another.

Human beings tend to become the norm that they are exposed to. This is the astonishing power of environment.

You become your surroundings!

Winning and Losing

If you are an athlete or an executive, you most likely have a desire for winning and an aversion for losing. Most will consider this completely normal.

A theme that you will find throughout this book is that while normal may be normal, but normal is NOT natural.

When the mind has a desire for one thing, it has an aversion for its opposite. In the case of winning and losing, the desire for winning is so great that it creates an anxiety about losing. An anxiety which often turns into outright fear.

Here is the crux of the matter: When the mind desires winning, its fear of losing far exceeds the desire for winning. As a result, there is intense anxiety. Which, in turn, sabotages the individual's performance. And often results in the very thing that the mind feared all along: Losing.

Does this mean that this anxiety always results in losing?

Of course not. But whether you win or lose, if your experience of the situation was filled with fear and anxiety, what have you really won?

The interesting thing is that the reason individuals wish to win is because of the feeling that it gives them. But in order to procure this "good" feeling, they spend the overwhelming majority of their time simmering in "painful" feelings.

Are three pounds of anxiety worth an ounce of peace?

Some individuals will say yes. And the reason that they will say yes is because they have been taught by society to be masochistic. That one must endure pain. That one must be "mentally tough." That the road to victory is paved with blood, sweat, and tears.

I would argue that victory is something one experiences everyday, if he immerses himself in the joy of his craft, and in his sincere quest for learning it. Blood, sweat, and tears are fine. But rather than bleeding from wounds, is it not better to bleed from passion? Rather than sweating from a maniacal adherence to "hard work," is it not better to sweat from an innocent immersion in one's craft? Rather than tears of pain, is it not better to have tears of joy?

If the individual would explore his mind and learn its propensities for desire and aversion, he would actually be victorious more often, precisely because the need to win would not sabotage his efforts. And the talent that he spent years amassing would be available to him when he needed it.

The same applies to all things in life. If we enter into any situation as a blank slate, we are able to deftly handle the situation. But if we enter the situation with likes and dislikes, fears and aversions, we become rigid and tense. And thus our speech and our actions lack wisdom.

If our aim remains fixed upon cultivating Atmamun, we will become observers of our feelings rather than "fixers" of them. We will be constantly vigilant of our observation and documentation of what feelings are arising within us, rather than allowing ourselves to react. Thus neither controlling the reaction nor refining it.

For reactions arise from a particular substrate. If that substrate is desire, then our reactions will be unruly. If it is observation of desire, then they will become wiser as time goes on.

Success Is A Product Of Innocence

It has often been the case throughout history that those who became legends in their fields were often recluses, loners, and misfits. They did not feel comfortable in crowds. They lived an almost hermetic existence. It is not coincidental that such a personality often achieves brilliance. For he is not Colored by the contagious mediocrity of a peer group.

Becoming a legend in your field, therefore, is very much about one's own nature and his comfort or discomfort in the world. We are taught that it is all about "hard work" and striving and ambition and blood, sweat, and tears. Yet there are literally countless examples of those in any field, particularly in sports, that are blessed with great talent but do not achieve success. Many of these individuals do "work hard." In fact, they often work "harder" than their contemporaries. But they still do not succeed. And we also know of those who don't put in nearly as much "work," and skip practice sessions, and do all of the things that we are told leads to failure. And yet they do succeed.

Why?

Success arises from innocence or from a sort of knowing. It arises from innocence when an individual is so devoted to his craft that he gives himself to it, day and night. Not because he wishes to make himself a success. But because the craft is quite literally a part of him. He simply cannot imagine doing anything else with his life. He feels that he is born to do it. He feels that this is what he was made for. And because of this intimacy with his craft and the innocence with which he approaches it, his skill level soars. And success comes running to him.

Then there are those who just know that they will be a success in their field. They can feel it. It is in their bones. They can see it. They can taste it. Not making it is simply not possible. Not because they talk themselves into it. Or because they think "positively." They genuinely scoff at the idea of not making it. This is not artificial. They truly feel this way in their heart of hearts.

The majority live in a world of hope and striving. They listen to the clichés and the endless motivational phrases that society tosses about. Hard work, striving, practice with a purpose, fake it till you make it, believe in yourself, walk the walk . . . These things are meant for those who need to be helped at every turn. They know within themselves that they are likely not going to make it. And in order to absolve themselves of this feeling, they do everything on the "outside" in order to make them feel differently on the inside.

I once wrote a discourse titled ***Hard Work Is No Excuse***. Hard work has become a scapegoat of sorts. It is a game that people play with themselves. They work "hard" in order to prove to themselves that When they don't make it, it just wasn't meant to be. Because if they don't make it Even With all of that hard work, what else could they have done?

Hard work never made anyone a success. It may have

played a catalytic role. But it was never the key to their success, regardless of what society says. It may have appeared this way. But it just isn't so. We have evidence before us all across the world of those who spend decades "working hard," but go nowhere.

Opponents of this claim will state that it is because they didn't work "smart." Or that they didn't "practice with a purpose." I myself was given to such ideas years ago. But life and my own experiences have taught me the truth.

Knowing comes first. Devotion and love come first. Hard work MAY come later. And for some people it never really comes at all.

I do not mean to suggest that one sits on the couch and success comes to him. What I am saying is that when endless striving and the toil and sweat are seen in the vicinity of great success, they are more methodology than the central key.

The man who knows that he will be a success makes "hard work" work for him. To him it is a tool in his arsenal. The man who does not know Works For hard work. He Relies upon hard work as the engine and the vehicle to get him there. And this latter instance rarely works.

The inside always trumps the outside. Knowing trumps belief. Innocence and sincerity are king.

The one who knows just knows. The one who doesn't know looks at "the odds."

The one who hopes for success creates backup plans,

"just in case." The one who knows has no need for a backup plan. Because he simply cannot imagine doing anything else with his life, he simply has no choice but to succeed.

Even among those who are successful, however, few become legends. For a successful man is one thing. A legend is something altogether different.

Legends are created from the inside rather than the outside. They are those who simply see things in a different way. They are often rebellious. They are not inhibited by the status quo. In fact, they seek to shatter it. And they feel comfortable with their ideas. Even though the world may ridicule them.

You see, society is against the creation of legends. This society is not meant for legends. It does not breed legends. It breeds clones. It breeds sheep. It values conformity. And hails mediocrity.

If you seek to be a legend in your field, it will help you to understand that you will have to be comfortable being an outcast. For you will not fit into this society. And if you do fit neatly into this society, there is no way that you will be a legend.

Society does not support anyone who goes against it. It only supports the masses. It supports common people with common thinking. And there is perhaps no greater contributor to mediocrity than the concept of "school." For education is one thing. School is another.

If you seek to be a legend, bring to the world something

that it has never before seen. There is something unique in you. For nature makes one-of-a-kind creations. Society makes clones.

Q: Dr. Gupta, I've always wanted to be exceptional at what I do. But I suffer from constant ups and downs. More downs than ups, actually. How do I overcome this and become a legend in my field?

KG: What do you do?

Q: I'm a professional golfer.

KG: What sort of downs are you speaking of?

Q: My scores are not where I want them to be. They are not consistent.

KG: If your scores are not consistent, then what this means is that the person who is producing the shots is not consistent. Would you agree?

Q: Oh, absolutely.

KG: From the standpoint of the execution of your shots, what do you believe is the reason for your inconsistency?

Q: I could say it's my swing. But I know it's probably my mind more than anything else.

KG: What do you mean by that exactly?

Q: I know that this is your domain. Don't you agree that it's probably my mind?

KG: That's much too broad a statement. Throwing

pebbles into the Atlantic ocean won't get us anywhere. What specifically do you believe is your problem?

Q: I really want to be great. I just don't know how to get there.

KG: Why, in your opinion, are you not already there?

Q: Basically because my tournament performances are not consistent enough.

KG: Where do you believe that performance comes from?

Q: I really don't know.

KG: I applaud your honesty. This will save us a lot of time. You see, performance is a side effect. And if you treat it as a goal, it will elude you.

Q: I've always been taught that performance is the main goal. I structured everything around it.

KG: How has this worked out for you?

Q: Not very well.

KG: Performance is a natural byproduct. If you understand the subtle nuances of training, performance simply comes to you.

Q: Can you explain that please?

KG: To be truly great, you must understand that the human body does not respond very well to goals or hopes or expectations. It responds to Perceptions. And the more clear cut your perceptions, the more consistent your results will be. Therefore, your entire training plan must be centered upon a foundation of perception rather than technique. Technique training is like a bullock cart. Perception training is like a Ferrari.

Q: So this perception training is what I'm lacking? I've never even heard of it.

KG: The truth is always rare. It is never found in the middle of the street. It is typically found in remote corners of the world. For it requires a true seeker to find it.

Q: That makes sense. So are you saying that everyone in professional golf is being trained wrong?

KG: I don't want to call it wrong or demonize anyone, for every coach tries to help his player in his own well-intentioned manner. I will just say that the manner by which professional golfers are taught is incongruent with the way that the human mind perceives and the human body responds. As a result, the player will constantly work against himself, rather than exploiting the natural gifts that nature has given him.

Q: And this is why so few players are consistent?

KG: True greatness and becoming a legend is very rare. And the fact that it is very rare is considered normal by the world, the society, the players, and the coaching establishment in professional sports. If you train against the natural grain of the human body, greatness will indeed be rare. If you train against the natural grain of the supernatural perceptive abilities of the human mind, greatness will be rare. In cannot be otherwise.

The Path To Atmamun

Whether something is possible or impossible is not your business.

Success and failure are ideas that will only serve as a burden to your quest.

Rather than finding the thing that you can imagine yourself becoming, find the thing that you simply cannot imagine yourself Not Becoming.

THE BURDEN OF THOUGHT

Descartes famously said, "I think, therefore I am."
I will say, "I think, therefore I am not."
Thinking is a tool that man can employ in order to carry out an activity or reach a particular goal. But it certainly doesn't Make the man. And for the vast majority of humanity, it is his undoing.

Thinking is a utilitarian activity. And, as such, it is very powerful. But the manner by which it is experienced by humanity has made man's life a prison.

Q: I've been blessed with intelligence. And my thinking is a part of that intelligence. How is it a burden?

KG: How do you use the lights in your home?

Q: I turn them on when I need them.

KG: And what if once you turned them on, you were not able to turn them off?

Q: I would waste electricity.

KG: And if the whole world did this, there would be a catastrophe.

Q: Yes.

KG: How do you use water in your home?

Q: I turn on the faucet when I need to use it.

KG: And you turn it off once you are done, I assume?

Q: Yes.

KG: What if you did not turn it off once you were done?

Q: I would waste thousands of gallons of water.

KG: And if the world did this, there would be an even greater water shortage than we have today. There would be a catastrophe.

Q: Yes.

KG: How do you use thought?

Q: Thoughts have given me many great ideas over the years. They've helped me do good things. And they've helped me succeed in my life.

KG: I don't dispute that. But when you are not thinking great ideas or good things, what are you thinking?

Q: I really don't know.

KG: Are you able to turn off this thinking like you turn off a faucet?

Q: I've never tried to.

KG: How do you drive your car? Please be honest. No one will judge you here.

Q: Sort of erratic.

KG: Please explain.

Q: I change lanes quite frequently. Trying to get to my destination as fast as I can.

KG: What are you mornings like?

Q: Like anyone's mornings I suppose.

KG: Please be specific.

Q: Fairly hectic. Getting the kids off to school. Running around looking for my keys, which seem to have legs of their own. It's definitely hectic.

KG: And how about work?

Q: Busy, busy. No downtime.

KG: And when you get home from work?

Q: Make dinner for the kids. Catch up on the work I didn't finish during the day. Get the kids to bed.

KG: How much peace do you know in any given day?

Q: Very little.

KG:How little?

Q: Most days, I have zero peace. That's for sure.

KG: When you are driving your car, you are in a rush to get somewhere, correct?

Q: Yes.

KG: When you sit, you feel the need to Do Something, correct?

Q: Yes. There is so much to do. It never ends.

KG: When you are here, you wish to be there. And when you arrive there, you seek to be somewhere else. Correct?

Q: Yes, but I don't just go there without a purpose. I go there in order to address my responsibilities.

KG: Yes, I understand. But please tell me this. When are you here without feeling any need whatsoever to go there?

Q: I suppose never. Because there is always something to do. The work and the chores never end.

KG: Do you believe that nature created you to do work and chores?

Q: No, but I can't carelessly leave my responsibilities.

KG: I understand that you are a responsible person. No one is doubting that. The first word in your response was No. Did you really mean No? Or was that simply a token gesture, so that you could get to the point you wanted to get across about taking care of your responsibilities?

Q: I suppose it was token. Because I've never thought of it.

KG: Let's think of it now. I ask you again. Do you believe that nature created you to do work and chores? Do you believe that nature created you to be a mule?

Q: It would be hard to believe that.

KG: How do you feel about the fact that you have little to no peace in your life?

Q: When you ask me point blank, I think it's terrible. But it's not high on my priority list when I'm faced with all the things I have to do in a given day.

KG: Thank you for your honesty. I will now ask you this.

The Burden Of Thought

If I gave you a deadline to complete all the chores and work that you had to complete and once that deadline was reached, you were never to do them again, would this work for you?

Q: No. The chores go on forever. And I have to work in order to live.

KG: It is true that one must work in order to make a living. And I'd like to say that you do an awful lot of work, but do you do any living?

Q: I suppose not.

KG: According to the logic that you have presented, the work and the chores and the running from here to there will never end. And you will continue to do them until you die. And you will die having lived as a mule. Never having known Peace.

Q: Isn't this just the way it is?

KG: Yes. For the person who accepts this deal.

Q: It's a rotten deal.

KG: Then why did you sign such a contract?

Q: I've never thought about it that way, I guess.

KG: Well, let's consider it now, shall we?

Q: Yes please.

KG: The reason that you run from here to there is not because of You. It is because of thoughts which tell you to do so. Your thoughts are always On. The lights are always on. And the faucet is never turned off.

Q: That's true.

KG: The thoughts run wild within you. Flying from here

to there. Thoughts about all things insignificant and foolhardy. It's a circus of never-ending thoughts. And while amidst this circus, a golden nugget appears in the form of a great idea, the vast majority of this thinking is degrading your constitution. And robbing you of all peace in your life.

Q: But why does this happen?

KG: Because of the nature of mind. Mind can exist everywhere. But it cannot exist Here.

Q: What do you mean?

KG: Mind is fundamentally a restless animal. This is its nature. It exists to roam. It thrives from jumping about. And its currency is thought. Shall I tell you a secret?

Q: Please.

KG: During those rare moments in your life that you were Here, you had clarity. You had joy. And the reason for this clarity and joy is because for that brief period of time that you were Here, you were free of thoughts. And because you were free of thoughts, you were free of the mind. You've always been told to fight for your freedom Of mind. But the truth is this: the greatest freedom in the world is freedom From mind.

The Path To Atmamun

If you *think* about something as you are looking at it, you will not have truly seen it.

Thought stands as a barrier between You and The Experience.

When one Experiences, there is no thought.
When there is no thought, there is no mind.
When there is no mind, there is Atmamun.

MINDFULNESS BINDS.
MIND_LESS_NESS LIBERATES.

The concept of mindfulness is in vogue.

But does it make sense? Isn't the fullness of the mind the entire problem? Are not the endless succession of thoughts the source of all misery?

The new age community has hung its colorful banners touting mindfulness. Institutions have been devoted to its propagation.

They advise that people should be "mindful" of every activity. To be here in the present. To inhibit the mind from drifting into the past or the future.

It is a wonderful concept. A sincere decree. A logical directive.

And wholly impractical.

Those who are so intent upon making You mindful are doing their best to avoid being mindful themselves.

What is wrong with the concept of mindfulness?

The tenets of mindfulness are very much like the tenets of all self-help philosophy. The principles that they espouse are sound and true. But the path that it recommends leads one astray.

Mindfulness Binds. MindLESSness Liberates.

If you visit the multitude of yoga centers, mindfulness retreats, meditation centers, and mindfulness institutions around the world, you will see people who are *Attempting To Be Mindful*.

While on the outside they give an appearance of serenity, the turmoil within rolls on. While on the outside there is stillness. On the inside there is restlessness.

You might argue that it is precisely because of this inner turmoil that they are attempting to be mindful. And you would be correct. But if you visit these same people ten years later, they will still be afflicted by the very same turmoil. Because mindfulness will not have worked.

If you were to follow the everyday lives of people who practice mindfulness you would notice that they are not enveloped in peace and tranquility.

Some who read these words will believe that I am condemning those who practice mindfulness. Actually, it is the opposite. The individuals who are given to ideas such as mindfulness are the rare individuals who seek to attain something truly worthwhile in their lives. They are Seekers. And my respect and sensibilities are perfectly in line with True Seekers.

Eastern concepts such as these have become diluted. And man is attracted by Form. The garb, the pose, the look, the walk . . . This has happened most famously with yoga. The yoga that is being practiced the world over, even in India where it originated, is a cosmetic production of deep-seated truths.

It is the same with meditation. And with mindfulness.

What is the trouble with mindfulness? And why doesn't it work?

The trouble with mindfulness is that it requires persistent effort. It is like attempting to empty the ocean with a teacup.

On the one hand you have the majesty of the mind. And on the other hand you have a human being who is trying to be "mindful."

Even the term "mindfulness" makes little sense. Isn't the entire problem a fullness of the mind? You are already Full Of Mind. What you want is to be Free Of Mind.

You don't want More mind. You want Less mind!

A far more accurate term is Awareness. This makes much more sense, does it not?

When you try to be "mindful," you are putting in constant effort to be "mindful." And the mind is coming at you with its torrents of thoughts, feelings, and emotions. The mind has been doing this for millennia. While you just started last year.

Who do you think will win this fight?

You will eventually tire. The mind will not. It doesn't matter for how long you try to be "present" or "mindful." Your efforts are no match for the ongoing engine of the mind. It is no match for the ocean of thoughts. It is no match for the mountains of emotion.

You will Tire Of Being Mindful. And the mind is well aware of this. The mind knows that as soon as you loosen your grip for even a fraction of a second, it will flood the senses as it has always done.

For how long can you keep hold of a tiger's throat?

Mindfulness is simply not sustainable. And thus it is impractical.

Is it not a more realistic solution to be Aware of one's lack of mindfulness?

I highly doubt that The Buddha was "mindful."

What he learned under the Bodhi Tree was not mindfulness, but Wakefulness.

Attempt to be mindful and you will remain asleep.

Become aware of the mind's patterns and you will awaken.

Those who are attracted by mindfulness do so because they have not been given another way.

Is there another way to achieve peace? Is there another way to cultivate equanimity?

Is there truly a way to become Awake?

Is it really and truly possible to become a living Buddha?

Yes. Absolutely. Without question.

What is it?

Atmamun.

The Path To Atmamun

If you are truly Sincere about achieving Freedom and Bliss, drop all techniques. For a technique will leave you bound to technique.

The How leads only to the How. It never leads to the destination of the How.

Stop playing games. Drop all solutions. Abandon all methodologies. Drop all slogans.

Do not jump on the bandwagon of ready-made solutions. For they will only take you further from the truth. And they will keep you entrenched in misery and bondage forever.

If you are truly sincere about achieving Freedom and Bliss, you will look directly at that which is preventing you from realizing them.

Ask yourself, what precisely is preventing you from having Freedom TODAY!

Ask yourself, what precisely is keeping you from Bliss right now!

Atmamun is a path away from All Paths.

It is a journey toward Questions rather than Answers.

Drop these disingenuous solutions . . .

Become a lone warrior . . .

And set off on a journey to the place within yourself that you have forever ignored.

NO-MIND: THE GATEWAY TO ATMAMUN

If there is a state of living enlightenment . . .

If there is a state of otherworldly bliss . . .

If there is an undeniable and fail-proof path to overwhelming peace . . .

It lies in the glorious state of No-Mind.

It is often more productive to first look at the obstacles to a goal than to directly look for a path to that goal. For if you find the obstacles, you find the path.

What is the obstacle to peace? What is the obstacle to freedom? What is the obstacle to equanimity? What is the obstacle to serenity? What is the obstacle to relaxation? What is the obstacle to joy? What is the obstacle to bliss?

Mind!

Mind stands as the single barrier between ourselves and the life that nature intended for us to live. Yes, the very same mind that commercials ask you not to waste. The very same mind which is the source of your pride. The very same mind that society tells you to "develop" and bolster and enliven.

Please understand this: in every society, in every nation

people are given the wrong information. The messages that humanity receives are either completely false, or they are so cryptic that it leaves far too much room for interpretation. Either way, they serve no purpose other than to cause man to lose his way.

There is no greater misunderstanding in this world, and thus no greater source of turmoil than that which concerns the true nature of mind.

Can the mind be a powerful force for good in a man's life? Certainly. But man never gets to this point. He rarely sees this face of the mind. He rarely benefits from its power. Rather, he lives forever under its thumb. And lives a life of slavery.

There is simply no greater enslavement in the history of man than man's enslavement to his own mind.

It matters not how much land a nation accumulates. It matters not how many wars it wins. It matters not how many tyrants it overthrows. The people of that nation will forever be enslaved by their own mind. And it is the sort of enslavement that no dictator can hope to match.

We are so enslaved by the mind that we don't even recognize that we are enslaved. The mind plays a magic trick upon us.

And the trick is so fantastic, so brilliant, so ingenious, that it enslaves a man whilst giving him the impression that he is free.

Our addictions and our vices are an example of our

enslavement to the mind. It is the mind that is addicted to things. And rather than challenge the addiction and refuse to do the mind's bidding, we ascribe the addiction to ourselves! We internalize it as a part of our "personality."

You have never been addicted to anything in your life. You have never had a single preference. You have never had any ideal. You have never had a single prejudice. You have never in your life had a single opinion. About anything!

But how can this be?

When you were a child, you were born a tabula rasa. And society could not help but to doodle its ideas upon you.

The ultimate teaching for any child would be to understand that fundamentally he is life itself. To teach him that his thoughts do not belong to him. The things that he becomes attracted to are not his attractions. The things that he craves are not his cravings. And that this is the only way to Freedom.

As one begins to explore and to look squarely at the mind, he begins to understand that he is Not The Mind! But this idea often leads to confusion and fright, rather than an immediate feeling of liberation.

The immediate reaction is the thought that if I am not the mind and I am not my thoughts and I am not my likes or dislikes and I am not my personality, who am I? I will relate to you that it is far more important at this stage to understand who you are Not. It will lead you to freedom much quicker if you learn who and what you are Not. For if you keep subtracting, there soon comes a time when you can subtract no more.

And when you reach this point you will discover who you are.

When your thoughts feel like imposters. And your ideas seem like noise. And your preferences fail to move you. And your pride is easily dropped. You will experience the state of No-Mind.

When you lose yourself in the activity you are involved in, and that which seemed to be an insignificant chore now seems like the only thing in the world, you will experience the state of No-Mind.

Some will say that such descriptions can also be indicative of mindfulness. And they will be correct. I do not disagree with the End Product of mindfulness. I disagree with the idea that mindfulness is a practical vehicle through which to reach this end product.

When we begin to viscerally understand that we are not the mind, we begin to look at the mind face to face. And for those moments that we look at the mind face to face, we have transcended the mind. For in order for you to look at something, you can only look at it if you understand that you are not it. Where there was one, there is now two. And this is the beginning of Atmamun.

The world has been trying to get you to control the mind. And calm the mind. And tame the mind. This is why it has spent billions on a campaign touting yoga and breathing and

No-Mind: The Gateway To Atmamun

meditation and mindfulness.

But it has not worked for the vast majority of people. No matter how much of these prescriptions they follow, they remain enslaved to the mind. And this leads to even more frustration.

Why has it not worked?

Because you have not been told the truth. You have only been shown a rosy path filled with flowery aphorisms. You have been taught to follow FORM. And ideas. And self-help jargon.

Would you like to know the truth?

Very well. Here is the truth: **The Mind Cannot Be Calmed Or Tamed. It Can Only Be Transcended!**

And it is transcended Not through activities. It is transcended through Understanding.

If you embark upon a sincere journey within yourself in order to understand all the things that you are not, you will have begun the path to transcending your mind. You will have begun to cut the ties that bind you to it. And you will have begun the path to the sort of freedom you have never before known.

It is only when you reach the point of No-Mind that you are then able to use the mind for your own purposes.

Understand very clearly that for as long as you are the mind, It will use you. And when you reach the state of No-Mind, you will be able to use It. And it will serve you the way it was meant to serve you. And in this state, the mind is the most powerful force in the world.

The Path To Atmamun

Once you get a taste of No-Mind, your personality will begin to deconstruct. The baggage that you have been carrying for decades will drop away.

And you will be see the world anew. You will soon be immersed in the Mind of the Spirit (Atmamun).

You will live in Clarity.

There will no longer be a veil or a filter between yourself and that which you see.

You will think when thoughts are needed. And you will use the mind when you need to use it for your own purposes.

You will Experience Life.

You will be Free.

You will be invested in Atmamun.

MEDITATION: WHAT YOU'VE NEVER BEEN TOLD

You have been told to spend twenty minutes a day in meditation. To take time out of your busy day to sit and breathe. Companies now have meditation rooms and yoga mats to avail their employees of a way to "de-stress."

As I've mentioned, society only has the capability to reveal partial truths. And a partial truth is just as harmful as a whole untruth. For it leads to greater frustration when the partial truths does not bear fruit.

I will also state candidly that partial truths would not be so readily published if there wasn't a market for them. The masses are unserious. And thus their appetite for unserious information is exploited.

Might sitting for twenty minutes of meditation give you a sense of peace? Certainly. For Those Twenty Minutes!

For when you resume your daily activities, you will succumb once again to your inner turmoil. Potions only work for a very short time. They are never a permanent solution.

If you are serious about truly accomplishing something in this domain, understand this: **Meditation Will Get You**

Nowhere. Meditativeness Will Give You The Keys To Your Inner Kingdom.

The unserious man puts in his obligatory twenty minutes of meditation in order to fulfill his daily quota. But the one who is truly serious transforms every single thing that he does into a meditation. In short, he becomes Meditative.

Brushing his teeth is a meditation. Putting on his clothes is a meditation. Driving to work is a meditation. Losing himself in his work is a meditation. Talking to his children is a meditation. Kissing them goodnight is a meditation. Washing the dishes is a meditation. Tapping keys on his computer keyboard is a meditation.

Everything Is A Meditation.

And when everything is a meditation, you have become Meditative. And when you have become meditative, there is nothing that is done reflexively. And when nothing is done reflexively, it is done perfectly.

This, my friend, is the key to human perfection.

Once again, the mindfulness folks will say that this sounds very much like mindfulness. Are they correct? Absolutely. I have never contested the End Product of what mindfulness touts. But I fully contest the idea that mindfulness is a practical vehicle to reach this end product.

When you "meditate" you are only in meditation when you meditate (and even that is questionable). When your life is Meditative, there is never a time when you are not in meditation.

Meditation: What You've Never Been Told

Meditation is Not an action. And the world has been taught to treat it as an action. And it is for this reason that it does not work for the overwhelming majority of practitioners.

Meditation is not about Doing something. It is not about Achieving something. It is not about Becoming something.

Meditation is about Allowing, rather than doing. It is about Stillness, rather than achievement. And it is certainly not about becoming something.

Please understand this: **Meditation Is About Becoming LESS Than You Ever Thought Possible.**

Meditation is about forgetting yourself. Meditation is about losing yourself. Meditation is about killing the meditator. For the moment the meditator dies, there is only the meditation. And when there is only the meditation there is complete peace.

If you train yourself to become what you are doing, you will be meditative. If you allow your activity to consume you whole, you will be meditative.

Herein lies the secret to creating Masterpieces. **The doer must disappear! For once the doer disappears, his masterpiece appears.**

The Path To Atmamun

The meditation that the world is taught to practice is all

about the "meditator." It is about the individual actively engaging in the practice of meditation. As such, it is a Doing.

But the truth is that exploration of the self is a subtle realm. It cannot be approached in a fashion similar to common tasks.

In this realm, the greatest currency is Sincerity. And the greatest tool is Surrender.

When any artist has had the performance of their life, it was because they happened to dissolve into the performance. They simply disappeared. And because they disappeared, there was no interference. As such, it became a meditative experience.

For as long as there is a "meditator" who is "meditating" nothing will happen.

Once the meditator disappears, all things suddenly become possible.

WORLD PEACE IS A COP OUT

Why do you hanker for world peace? What does peace among nations have to do with you?

There is so much turmoil in your own life, and so many fires in your day to day existence, of what concern to you are the fires that go on around the world?

Man is very clever. He attaches himself to high-minded ideals in order to avoid doing the work that needs to be done. He convinces himself that he is worldly and progressive and magnanimous by hanging on the coat-tails of societal principles. All the while, his own life lies in shambles.

The greatest thing that you can give to the world is peace in your very own life.

If you wish to play games, by all means play them. But at least be honest enough to admit this to yourself. Admit to yourself that it is simply too painful to work through the conflicts and the disappointments that pepper your daily existence. Admit to yourself that you don't have the appetite for the arduous work of attaining inner peace. Then you will be free to pick up your picket signs in protest of this and that.

Man loves nothing more than to avoid the immediate. He loves nothing more than to abandon the practical in exchange for the romantic. He continually flows toward the path of least resistance. And it is for this reason that he achieves nothing worthwhile in his life.

Drop this idea of world peace and set off on a journey toward inner peace!

Forget world hunger and for the first time in your life seek to satisfy the deepest hungers you've had for yourself!

World peace is simply a manifestation of the lack of one man's peace. And for as long as man seeks to "correct" the world, he will gain nothing and lose himself.

Your parents, your advisors, and all of society has told you to be "unselfish." Selfishness has become a terrible slur. You are told to help others and love thy neighbor as thyself.

I understand that these ideals sound good. But have you ever sought to examine them for their validity?

May I ask you a question? Unless you address your own issues, how will you have the wisdom to help another man with his issues? Unless you have settled things in your own home, what credibility do you have in helping your neighbor? And for as long as you continue to look at others because you have been taught to be "unselfish," when will you acquire the "selfishness" necessary to look at your own issues and your own needs?

For I promise you this: Unless things are in order in your life, you are in absolutely no position to help another.

If every man and woman were encouraged to address their own needs and their own issues and faults, we would have a society filled with wisdom rather than a society filled with ideals.

The way to help the world is to help yourself. Not in the form of indulgence, but in the form of self-examination. Not in the form of gluttony, but in the form of self-reflection.

Man's greatest gift to man is also his greatest gift to himself: The gift of becoming Whole.

The Path To Atmamun

If you are serious about living a peaceful life, drop all matters pertaining to the world, and pursue all matters pertaining to yourself.

The state of the world will do nothing for you. The state of your interiority will do everything for you.

Your greatest protection from the world is also your greatest gift to the world: Your Personal Peace.

A fraction of daily peace in your own life will benefit you more than any sort of "world peace."

PARENTS DO NOT RAISE CHILDREN

Parenting is the most arduous role that human beings are asked to assume. It is the most eye-opening, exhilarating, and tumultuous ride of a human being's life.

It is tumultuous because we believe that we are to raise the child. This is not true. Parents do not raise children.

Nature does.

Nature does not make mistakes with children. Parents do.

But there is one mistake that nature has made with adults. And that is to allow the biology of childbirth to be granted to all adults.

This one fact has led to more catastrophe and human suffering than all the world wars combined.

A child is such a sacred creation that nature should not have allowed him to be handled by just anyone.

A child is such a grand possibility that nature should not have allowed his potential to be destroyed by the hand of man.

The ancient saints of the Himalayan order say that liberation does not come to just anyone. It comes to the very few.

Parents Do Not Raise Children

For it requires lifetimes of cultivation of certain inner conditions. And when these are met, liberation comes.

Nature was so careful with liberation. But it has been so careless with children.

I will state outright that unless a parent has achieved a certain degree of wisdom, nature should not allow them to have children. Their physiology should be rendered non-functional.

The vast majority of human beings in the world, myself included, should not have been granted nature's permission to have children. For this is the sort of on-the-job training that is completely unfair to the child.

Most adults have not raised themselves yet. They have not understood themselves yet. They have not come to terms with their own deficiencies. They have fundamentally unresolved issues. They don't know who they are.

How can such a one possibly raise a child?

The concept of "children having children" does not simply apply to teenage pregnancy. It applies to the vast majority of human beings having children, regardless of their age.

You see, a child is a mirror. The most stark and unflinching mirror in existence. And when the parent looks at his child, subconsciously he sees his own inadequacies. And in seeing his own inadequacies, he cannot bear the pain of them. As a result, he attributes the inadequacies to the child.

And it is at this juncture that all the troubles begin. For it as at this juncture that he decides to do something that will change the course of both of their lives: He attempts to Fix the child!

He attempts to correct him. And mend him. And improve upon him.

And in doing so, he destroys him.

A parent doesn't have the wisdom to see beyond his own ego. And he becomes intoxicated with this newly granted power. This new found control.

And this becomes his undoing. For he abuses his power. And assumes omniscience over the child's life. He teaches him "lessons." And tells him what to think. And indoctrinates him into religions.

He has taken this child who has come into this world colorless, and painted him with the colors of his religion and his nation's flag.

If a man or a woman is wise, they will look at their children in a completely different way. They will stop teaching and begin listening.

Why?

Who is the most joyful person in any family? The small child? Or the grown adult?

In the family unit, there is the adult who is miserable and disappointed and stressed and confused. And there is a child who is energetic, full of life, joyful, and playful.

Let me ask you something: Who should learn from whom? Should the parent teach the child to be miserable? Or should he learn from the child how to be joyful?

The child sees everything as new. He sees everything as if it is the first time he has ever seen it. The adult hasn't seen a new thing in years.

Should the adult teach the child the academic and stale information about this old and uninteresting thing? Or should he learn from the child what he himself has been missing for all these years?

You can refer to all of the "parenting" tips that fill the popular magazines if you like. But these will only address Behavior.

But behavior is never the way to address an issue. To address an issue from the standpoint of behavior is like addressing the problems of a tree at the level of the branch, rather than at the level of the root.

Behavior, whether in the child or the adult, is the natural byproduct of the person's outlook, perception, and level of understanding. If you address these more fundamental elements within the human being, the behavior will change by itself.

If you wish to raise wise children, stop being a parent. Abandon the idea of ownership. For whatever a man owns, he destroys.

Do you not see that you treat other people's children far better than you treat your own?

Why?

Because you don't own them. But the children that you

own are the very ones that you take for granted.

The truth is that you don't own your children. Parents are owned by their children far more often than their ego and their delusions allow them to accept. Parents are enslaved by their need for their children to do well. And this causes an enormous amount of pain in their lives.

Parents are enslaved by the need for their children to reflect well on the family name. And this produces an incalculable amount of strife.

The truth of truths is what every parent will deny to their dying day. But perhaps in their old age they will finally allow themselves to admit the most painful truth of their parenting lives. The one that they forever refused to allow themselves to entertain. Because the fear was too profound. And the pain was too great.

What is that truth?

Whatever a parent does in the name of his or her child, he is really doing for himself.

Feel free to let loose your mock outrage. Scream at me for speaking such an unspeakable lie. Do what you will.

And while you are lost in your fit of rage, I will calmly ask you: How many hours out of every day of your family life are filled with Peace? How many days out of every month are completely free of family conflict? How many days out of every week are free of family turmoil?

I do not mean to demonize you. Understand, my friend,

that the accusations that I level against you I have first leveled against myself a thousand times over.

Parenting is a role that the vast majority of human beings are simply not ready for. Because they have not attained to their own wisdom, they are simply not equipped to become a role model of wisdom for their children.

And understand this: A child does not need a parent's teaching. He needs a parent to create for him a certain environment. And this environment will do all of the teaching necessary.

If you create an environment of peace, the child will learn to be relaxed.

If you create an environment of understanding, the child will be open with his problems.

If you create an environment of silence, the child will become averse to the world's noise.

If you create an environment of freedom, the child will have the courage to find his own way.

But in order for a parent to do this, he will have to first learn these things for himself.

And once he does, he will be drawn less to the control and the ego of parenting, and more to the creation of an environment that will allow the child to never lose his way.

The parent's ultimate duty is to not make the child dependent upon him.

The parent's ultimate duty is to allow the child to never

lose sight of himself.

Imagine This . . .

Imagine that tomorrow morning, your child was going to leave the home.

Imagine that you were going to drive him to the airport. And as you were driving him to the airport you sat in complete disbelief that this time actually came.

Somewhere within the common sense part of your brain you knew that this day was going to come.

Didn't you?

Yes and no.

You knew it Theoretically. But it was so far off that you never considered it a true possibility.

Imagine that you are driving him to the airport NOW.

You are thinking of all the years that have passed. The nuances, the joys, the quiet times, and the conflicts.

And you suddenly have this urge to rewind the clock.

You have this painfully desperate wish to have just two years of that time returned to you. Even two months . . .

But the universe says to you, "I'm truly sorry. But you've had your time. And now that time is gone."

What you wouldn't give for another shot. What you wouldn't give for a handful of borrowed time.

You think to yourself, "My goodness . . . All the time that

you wasted. So many years flushed down the drain."

And now it is time to reap the benefits and the sorrows of what you spent decades planting. All of those times when it was All About YOU. All of those times that you sat on your pedestal and preached your silly doctrines. All of those times that you were so busy "teaching" that you didn't have the time to Listen.

Being a parent is, in many ways, a burden. The burden of possessing too much power. And any human being that is given too much power, even though he may have the best of intentions, ends up abusing it.

I now bring you back to the present. You now have the time that you begged for.

What the universe couldn't give to you, I'm giving to you now.

And as you run forward into this rediscovered life, I hope that you will be acutely cognizant of the fact that **The Day Is Coming!**

Parents Don't Really Love Their Children

Do you love your children?

Love is such an easy word, isn't it? Four letters that just slip off the tongue. It's used just as often as hello and goodbye.

And frankly, in the context of modern life it means about as much.

If you have children, you don't love them. You control the times they sleep and wake. You control the things the say, the manner in which they say them, and even the tone with which they are said.

You plan their future for them. You make them ask your permission for the most menial privileges. You control their behavior by withholding your affection (I will not call it love). You tell them not to embarrass you.

You have free reign to speak to them anyway you like because you know they will be quick to accept your apology. While you are slow to accept theirs.

There is so little resistance, so little caution, when you speak to them because you are the King and they are the servants. Until the day comes when they are ready to leave home. And for the first time in your life you realize that it is you who now stands begging them not to leave.

The problem with being a parent is that there is too much power. And it is in the nature of human beings to abuse any power that they have been given unchecked.

You treat them the way you do, not because you feel that you should. But because you Can!

You treat them the way you do because you are lost in yourself. You are lost in your own little world of conflicts that have lived with you for years.

You do not love them. Not because you don't wish to. But because you have not yet come to that moment in your life when you see your life as meaningless. And meaningless it is.

When your life becomes meaningless. When you can

live, instead of asking from life, you will have the capacity to give love. And it will look far different than it does now.

The fundamental tenet of love is Freedom.

The one who gives love has no need to control. He sees the humanity in the human being. And he loves him for who he is.

He has no need to meddle. For how can one meddle with perfection?

And, on a practical level, if some rules need to be set for the well-being of the child, they are set. But they are set in clay rather than stone. And they are set with the child rather than against him.

For your entire life, you feel that you have given so much to your children. But you have failed to give them that which they have craved from the moment they were born.

They did not need you to buy them things. They did not need for you to take them places. They did not need for you to raise them or teach them.

What they needed was for you to be so madly in love with them, that they would never feel the need to leave you.

What they needed was for you to look into their eyes and see creation.

What they needed was for you to give your entire self to them, and keep your mind to yourself.

There is still time . . .

Despite all that you have done, they will still accept you.

Do not kiss them on the cheek. Or tell them your lies about loving them. Or fill them with your high-minded advice.

Lose yourself in their eyes. And fall completely in love with who they are.

Allow them the privilege of feeling that they are worthy of such love. Allow them the intoxication of feeling that they are perfect beings.

In losing yourself in their eyes you will give them the love that they have always given to you. And nothing will need to be said.

For what sort of love is a love that can be reduced into words?

A Letter For Your Children

Dear Child,

I have so much to apologize for. And I know that an apology is simply not enough. But it marks a new beginning for the relationship that binds me to you.

I'm sorry for the times I hurt your heart, for I was blinded by my ego.

I'm sorry for the times I saw your tears, but not your heartfelt pain.

I'm sorry for the times I considered you less than me, for I was intoxicated by my role as a parent.

I'm sorry for the times I ignored you, for I took you

completely for granted.

I'm sorry for the times I hugged you loosely, while you hugged me tight.

I'm sorry for the times I showed you my hand, instead of extending it.

I'm sorry for the times I spoke to you without looking at you.

I'm sorry for the times I expected you to give, not realizing that this was what you had been doing all along.

I'm sorry for asking from you the things that you knew not how to give.

I'm sorry for holding grudges, when you forgave so easily.

I'm sorry for teaching you lessons, when I should have been learning them.

I'm sorry for scolding you for things that I incited in you.

I'm sorry for not looking at who you were, instead of who I wanted you to be.

I'm sorry for throwing away those precious, lovely years.

As I look at you now, I see the years in your face. And I vow not to waste another day.

I now understand that it is I who must learn from you.

And while I have no right to expect it, may you have pity on this person who was so blinded by his role as a parent, that he could not see the child in front of him.

And now I am ready to look into your eyes and listen

with all of my heart.

For I now understand that you have always had what I have always longed for.

The Worst Thing That A Parent Can Give

Parents are in the habit of giving too much to their children. And most of what they give is not only detrimental to the child's growth, but it interferes in his development as an individual.

The worst thing that a parent can give to his child is his Mind.

The child's mind is far superior to that of the parent. This is because it is not well developed. A well developed mind is simply a trash bin that is more full. The more empty the trash bin, the less the trash.

In giving his mind to his child, the parent passes on to him all of his prejudices. He passes on to him the way in which he perceives the world.

The child is barely born and the parent stands in wait with a suitcase full of advice. The child does not need your advice. Or your help. Or your direction.

The greatest thing you can do for your child is to not interfere.

It is the most difficult thing in the world for a parent to do. But it is also the most important.

Parents Do Not Raise Children

The mind is the greatest burden known to man. And the less of yours you give to him, the less burdened he will be.

And unfortunately, the place where the mind can have such a disastrous influence on someone else . . .

The place where human beings have complete access to the sensibilities, the thoughts, and the fears of another . . .

The place in which control of another human being's life is a most seductive proposition . . .

The place in which emotions, desires, expectations, and guilt are intricately woven into the very foundation . . .

The place in which the influence of one human being upon another can be detrimental or inspirational. Sometimes neither. But often, both . . .

The place that has become the most dangerous place in the world . . .

Is the Family!

The family is a place in which mind collides with mind. Each searching for its own place. Each longing for its own freedom.

But what is not understood is that that which seeks freedom is the very thing that produces enslavement.

What makes the concept of family so cumbersome is that every member of the family is lost in a search for something. What makes the family so dangerous is that none of the members knows what precisely it is he is searching for.

This search, this endless groping, causes the members of

the family to collide with one another. Each member searching for something, not With the other members, but Through them.

The family must be understood for what it is. The members must understand their true state of spiritual evolution. Those who realize this can truly impart wisdom. For them, the family becomes a haven.

For those who believe that they know, for those who believe that they are in control, suffering is the order of the day. And endless conflict the staple of their lives.

And it all begins with understanding that one is not their mind.

In understanding this, the parent begins to hold his opinions and ideas loosely.

And once the parent lives in freedom from their own ideas and prejudices, his children will be able to live free from them as well.

The Child Must Raise The Parent

Adults have turned into *parents*. And children have become their slaves.

The problem with parents is they think that they know. Perhaps they once knew. But that which they once knew is long gone. And that which was worth knowing has long been forgotten.

The parent lives in the world of yesterday. He hopes for

tomorrow.

> The child has no hope. For him, tomorrow is an illusion.
> The child lives. The parent dreams.
> The child is raw. The parent is calculated.
> The child is spontaneous. The parent is rehearsed.
> The child lives. The parent makes a life.
> If there is someone to be inspired by, who should it be?
> The one who is conditioned? Or the one who is free?
> If there is someone to learn from, who should it be?
> The one who searches for answers? Or the one who has

no need for them?

The Path To Atmamun

Look into your children's eyes and see all of creation.

This is all that needs to be done.

For seeing them in this way will give them all the love they will ever need.

And they will grow up in the glorious atmosphere of Atmamun.

YOU ARE FAST ASLEEP

You do not live in the real world. You live in the world of Mind. You live in the world of Thought.

Understand what I am about to say. And understand it clearly. For it is not a sleight against you. It is simply the unadulterated truth:

You Are A Schizophrenic.

Your existence is such that you live your entire day within a cocoon of ceaseless thought. Your mind rambles endlessly. It produces thoughts. Thoughts produce feelings. And you react to those feelings.

And this entire escapade occurs within You. There is no reality to speak of. It is only the semblance of reality.

You hear voices. And your entire life is lost in a frantic quest to quell some voices and accentuate others.

This is the plight of all humanity.

You are not unintelligent.

You Are Simply Asleep.

What does it mean to be Asleep?

It means that reality is lost upon you. You live forever in

You Are Fast Asleep

thoughts of past and future. You hope. You dream. You lament. You ponder.

You never deal with What Truly Is. You deal only with what your Mind Tells You What Is.

As a result, you are a walking zombie. You drive to work, and you don't remember how you got there.

You place your keys on the nightstand and you don't remember placing them there.

You speak a dozen words to your neighbor and you don't remember speaking them.

Your live your entire life in a state of Eventually. You live forever looking deep into the distant horizon. And every ship that crawls upon the horizon generates a hope in you. A hope that this is the ship you've been waiting for.

And if this is not your ship, then you await another. And as you wait, your life passes you by.

I've devoted my life to Awakening.

Awakening myself, and awakening those gloriously talented souls who seek my counsel. These individuals have the world at their feet. Fame. Money. Accomplishment.
But they lay asleep within their bed of riches.

This is why they seek "more."

What they eventually come to understand is that the reason that they have not achieved satisfaction or contentment or equanimity or peace or bliss is because such things cannot be achieved through "success."

They can only be achieved through Awakening.
How does one Awaken?
By first understanding that he is asleep.

The Path To Atmamun

Virtually everything that you do every single day of the week is done automatically and reflexively.

You quite literally sleepwalk through your life.

But before you ask me "how to awaken," you must acquire a heartfelt understanding of what I'm trying to tell you.

Catch yourself in this sleepy state. See with wide open eyes how asleep you truly are. Notice that everything you do is completely reflexive.

And then you will be primed to Awaken.

And there is nothing that can transform the life of a sleepy man more than Awakening to Atmamun.

YOU HAVE EVERYTHING, BUT DO YOU HAVE PEACE?

It is often the case that human beings fail to see things not because they are too far, but because they are right under their nose.

In working with celebrity clients, for example, I have found that it is almost always the case that they spend their careers chasing something. But upon acquiring it they are filled with the need to begin a new chase.

The world thinks they have everything. But they themselves feel a sense of emptiness.

Upon completing their ascent to the top of the mountain, they believe they will see a vista of Truth. But, in fact, what they often discover is an endless landscape of mountain ranges.

This is the predicament of all humanity.

Human beings have become accustomed to chasing mirages. And this is why their thirst is never quenched.

And they have chased for so long that they have become accustomed to the chase.

There is a chase in the morning. A chase in the evening. A chase at work. A chase with the children. A chase for achievement.

It is only when he or she discovers that the chase is Fruitless . . .

It is only when he or she discovers that there is nothing to Find . . .

It is only when he or she discovers that, in fact, the chase is not a running Toward something, but a running Away from something . . .

That clarity begins to dawn.

Enlightenment is not an achievement. For it does not come to the ambitious.

Peace is not an eventuality. For it is only available NOW.

What is it that humanity is running from?

When distilled into the most basic truth, it is a fact that man's greatest fear is not what may come. Or what may not. It is not death. And it is not failure.

Man's greatest fear is his fear of HIMSELF.

Man will complain to the heavens about the details of his miseries. But if you attempt to remove them from him, he will fight to the death in order to preserve them.

Why?

Because he is unsure of who he might be without them.

If you lead him by the hand to a world of peace, he will hesitate. For what will he do without a world of turmoil?

It is his greatest ploy to beg for peace on the one hand,

You Have Everything. But Do You Have Peace?

and deny it fully with the other. For peace is a dangerous word for him.

And bliss can only be handled in small doses.

It is for this reason that I always explain to my clients that I will not attempt to bring them to a world of Pure Peace all at once. They will be able to retreat from it at will.

But for those rare ones who have seen through the mirage . . .

For those who have finally come to the realization that this world really has nothing to offer them . . .

We walk toward Peace in big bold steps. For they are finally ready for it.

They are ready to live in a world without the anticipation of expectation, or the false whispers of empty hope.

And when they arrive there, they laugh. They laugh, not necessarily because of the joy that they feel, but because of the complete absurdity that was the foundation of their previous existence.

It was all so simple, they say.

And it was so close. They were never far from it. But they had never before been ready for it.

Understand this: **Your Mind Will Never Spare You.**

For it has not spared any man.

It will chatter incessantly. It will rob you of your equanimity. It will entice you into petty squabbles. It will burden you with guilt. It will show you grand imaginings. And fill you with the fear of not achieving them.

It will give you a false identity. And show you a face in the mirror that you one day will not recognize.

It is a master of creation. It has, in fact, created You!

And in identifying yourself with the persona that it has given you, you will live a life of PAIN.

What is the way out?

Are you ready for Instant Peace?

Dear friend, do not be quick to answer this question. For if your response rolls of your tongue with ease, it is likely a reflexive response. And if you respond reflexively now, you will shy away at the critical moment.

You wear many faces. Some you show to the world. Some you keep hidden in the closet. And some you cannot bear to reveal even to yourself.

Behind all of these faces there is a human being. And behind the human being is the Face-less Consciousness.

No matter how beautifully you wear the face of your choice, the wearer will always be more than the worn.

Shall I tell you the secret to Peace?

I will provide for you the writing on the front door. But, as in all things, the magic is in the EXPERIENCE.

Here it is:

When You Disappear, Your Problems Will As Well.

What do I mean?

When you say "I", who is the I that you are speaking

of? And who is this entity that says "I"? From where does this voice arise? And whom is it referring to?

Therein lies the exploration.

If you continue to live your life as one of your faces, you will never achieve peace.

Why?

Because it is this very face that robs you of it.

Equanimity. Enlightenment. Peace. Nirvana. Moksha. Samadhi. Mushin.

These can never be available tomorrow. For tomorrow doesn't exist. They can only be gotten NOW.

And they are only available to the one who has finally Had Enough. They are only available to the one who is willing to throw away All Of His Faces.

They are available to the one who is willing to exchange his identity of being Something in return for becoming Nothing.

And when a man becomes nothing, he instantly becomes Everything!

Freedom From The Mind

If you examine the last 20 years of your life, you will find that it is saturated with disappointments and fears and conflict. It is not your fault. And it is not the fault of those with whom you were in conflict.

It was not about who was right. Or who was wrong. It

was not about logic. Or reason. Just unbridled emotion.

Truth be told, there is great solace to be found in misery. There is comfort in pain. A part of us enjoys playing the lead role in our drama.

But we pay for it with our lives.

We live reactive and reflexive lives. Spinal and emotional reflexes prevail. And this is not living. To choose to let our drams drift away for good is a difficult choice to make. To walk away from our misery is a very difficult thing to do.

I assure you I am not being facetious. I speak with complete seriousness. For these miseries and turmoils and complexities and conflicts have lived with us for so long that they have become a part of us. And to remove them from our lives leaves a hole that we do not know how to fill.

Man is an amazingly adaptive creature. He can become accustomed to simply anything. And once he becomes accustomed to something, be it joy or misery or pain, he becomes comfortable within it.

If he vacillates between happiness and misery, he becomes accustomed to the vacillation. But there are those who finally reach the day in which they say: Enough is Enough. And they ready themselves for a brand new journey. A journey that is no longer about taking sides.

A journey that values the sanctity of the relationship more so than the ego of the individual.

Mind you, it is not about "swallowing one's pride." It is

You Have Everything. But Do You Have Peace?

about understanding that there is no pride to speak of. There is only a surrender to the innocence and sincerity of the relationship.

The relationship between two human beings. The relationship between a human being and himself. The relationship between himself and his life.

The greatest thing to understand is that our reactions are completely the result of us living wholly within the mind. The mind takes sides. The mind enjoys conflict. And the mind enjoys resolution.

The mind simply enjoys the game and the drama. The mind enjoys pain, perhaps because it enjoys setting up the guilt and the reconciliation that follows.

But if we see the drama as a drama that is independent of ourselves, then we begin to break away from the drama. We begin to quite easily surrender our ego at the door. And this becomes a completely painless and natural phenomenon once we stop functioning from the Place Of Mind.

Wisdom is the understanding that we have bought into a game. That none of it is real. And that we have become pawns on a stage. Pawns of the mind.

This very realization is the path to liberation.

Even if you have this understanding, the understanding will still be fresh and "intellectual" in the beginning. And thus conflicts will continue to arise.

But they will become less frequent. And shorter in duration.

And one day they will stop altogether.

They will not stop because we have run away from them.

They will stop because we no longer need them.

Our World Of Problems

We find ourselves constantly putting out fires.

When we are not putting out fires, we are thinking about the ones that may come. And we are lamenting the ones we have lived through.

We have fire all around us. And it is in the center of this inferno that our life moves.

We have a problem with the way our kids treat us. The way the waitress speaks to us. The way our spouse scolds us. The way our job makes us feel. The way our boss makes us work. The way the cold makes us tremble. The way the heat makes us sweat. The way the car delays to start. The way our hair fails to part.

This is the way it goes for us.

And the most tragic part of this is that we fail to realize it. We are given ridiculous adages such as "That's life."

Instead of examining the totality of the situation, we are told to become better problem solvers. The magazines, the journals, the books, and the media devote their content to so-called experts who give us tips on how to better solve our problems.

You Have Everything. But Do You Have Peace?

Do you want to be a better fireman? Or do you wish to free yourself from the inferno?

The wrong question is being asked (it always is, isn't it?). And believe me, friend, it is always about the question rather than the answer.

The question is NOT "How do I solve my problems?'

The question is "Why do I have problems in the first place?"

But who asks such a question?

The only person who would ask such a question is the person who rejects the stories that he has been told. The silly little tales about life being difficult and stressful and that in order to make our way through it we must deal with its wrath.
That "life is not a bowl of cherries."

To say that it is not a bowl of cherries is to imply that it is a bowl of something.

If to you, life is a bowl . . .

If to you, life is a container of any sort . . .

Then this implies that you are living INSIDE OF IT.

And if you live inside of something you will get bruised with every bump in the road. You will become dizzy with every roll. You will simply be a pebble in a container.

No one ever told you that you could be free of the container. No one ever told you that there was a world outside of it.

They told you to man up and accept the bruises. And

they started giving you tips on how to tend to your wounds.

They told you that life is full of dangerous flames. And they started giving you advice on how to spend your entire life putting out the fire.

And there you have sat, thimble in hand, tossing three drops of water into a raging inferno.

If this is not the way, then what is the way?

What is one to do?

My friend, fire never harmed anyone. It only harmed those who chose to get in its way.

Let the flame burn. Let the problems amass. Let the feelings of ill will flow through you. Let the boss yell and the children scream.

The very attempt to distinguish the flame will only make it burn brighter.

This flame is simply life being life. And the reason we get burned is because we attempt to put our arm around it and call it Ours.

Let life be life. Allow events to carry on of their own accord. Live alongside them. But do not intersect with them.

In looking at life as life, you will move freely in the world. You will do what the moment requires and not an ounce more. You will give what the situation asks of you and you will not be attached to it.

Let the flame burn to the heavens.
And do not try to find your reflection in it.

Live as a man who roams the endless deserts. And who sails the seven seas. Without any attempt at navigation.

Allow the delicate hand of instinct to lead you, for in it lies the truest of truths.

Life is jagged and raw. And by attempting to Own It you turn it into a problem.

Watch the flame rise. Use it to warm yourself on a cold day.

And as you watch it, it will eventually begin to see its reflection.

In You.

All Our Dramas

If you are alive you will have troubles. This will never end. You will have them until your dying day.

It doesn't matter how you deal with it, or how you look at it, or turn lemons into lemonade or any such silliness. Trouble is trouble. Problems are problems. And they will be at your throat for as long as you live.

Almost every single day of your life there will be a running soap opera of some sort. Perhaps a new problem or one that keeps recurring. And the most intuitive thing to do is to try to resolve the problem. To put an end to the soap opera.

But this doesn't work.

Why?

Because although you try to end the soap opera with one hand, you start a new one with the other. You don't have any real desire to end your soap operas. You can't live without them.

You enjoy them. They add meaning to your life. They are like pieces of your jewelry. They play a significant part in your life.

You only pretend to not want them.

You Relish your problems. And this is why they never go away. You will make certain of this.

You enjoy the times of sorrow. You feel a sense of comfort when you cry. Wallowing in guilt is a delicacy. Playing the victim is a luxury.

If someone tried to take these things away from you, they would have a fight on their hands.

All your problems, your disappointments, your guilt, your worries, your miseries, your pain, your sorrow, your apprehensions, and anxieties could disappear in an instant. But where would that leave you? Who would you be without them? What would you do with your time?

I am not saying that you Should let go of these things. I am saying that they exist because you invite them.

And since this wasn't enough to muddy the circumstances of your life, you have now added a new level of complexity by stating that you want to get rid of them. This will keep you busy forever. And this is what you are seeking to do.

Human beings have a habit of creating problems for

themselves in order to add meaning to their lives.

And the reason they seek meaning is because they have not lived life at all.

The Path To Atmamun

Be truthful. Be sincere. Do you really want to be rid of your problems?

If so, then understand that why it is that you hold on to them.

The reason that you have problems is because you gain something from them. And unless the perceived gain from Peace exceeds the perceived gain from Misery, you will forever live in misery.

Man gets what he wants.

The reason that he is where he is, is because it is okay for him to be there.

HAPPINESS WILL MAKE YOU MISERABLE

Man is not searching for happiness. He is running from sadness.

He believes that happiness is the opposite of sadness. When, actually, there are only shades of difference between them.

Happiness and sadness are moods. Moods are a byproduct of thought. And thought is the very constitution of the mind.

The unenlightened man thinks, and he then responds to the feeling which arises from the thought.

And then matters become even more complex. He begins to have a thought about the thought. And he begins to have an opinion about the feelings. He categorizes his feelings into likes and dislikes. And he attempts to find ways to cultivate the good feelings and avoid the bad ones.

Thus begins his frantic search for "happiness."

It is at this stage where the world of self-help, positive thinking, and motivational recipes come into existence. Books are written and articles are generated outlining ways to attract the good feelings and avoid the bad ones.

Prescriptions abound. Slogans and bumper stickers

Happiness Will Make You Miserable

and "Ten ways to" lists flood the public consciousness.

The majority of the writings argue that since feelings come from thought, then why not think positive thoughts?

Others recommend singing a song, doing something kind, turning off your phone, taking a walk, practice smiling, taking a vacation . . .

Do such things work?

They can.

Why?

Because the mind is an ephemeral element. It changes moods and preferences with every third breath.

But that is not the real question.

The real question is, How long does the good mood or the positive feeling last?

The tide always returns, does it not? Cosmetic fixes will always lead to results equally cosmetic.

While that may be the real question, the most important question is this: How satisfied are you with your current state of affairs?

Happiness and misery are two sides of the very same coin. To seek one is to seek the other.

The only way out is bliss. Bliss is beyond both happiness and sadness. For it is not dependent upon a fortuitous event or an enjoyable circumstance.

It is a byproduct of wisdom. The wisdom that comes from seeing things the way they truly are. The wisdom that comes from seeing the world the way that it truly is. The wisdom that comes from understanding that life is not what we think it is.

Bliss is The Way.

It is the search that ends all searches.

The Path To Atmamun

The search for happiness is nothing more than a reaction to unhappiness. As always, the truth is a function of subtraction rather than addition.

Happiness and misery are different segments of the same wave. Neither of them will benefit you.

Bliss is the abandonment of the search for happiness. And the abandonment of the search for pleasure.

For this will return you to the moment that you forever seek to escape.

BLISS IN AN INSTANT

Do you want instant bliss? I will not keep you in suspense. I will give you the secret right at the beginning.

Understand that when I reveal it to you, you will say that you already know it. But I will argue fiercely that you do not.

I will argue that you know it in your head. But you do not know it in your heart. The knowing of the head is for cocktail parties. The knowing in the heart is for transformation.

Are you ready for the secret to instant bliss?

Here it is: **You Are Going To Die!**

This is not a theoretical understanding. Or some far off possibility.

It is the heartfelt realization that stabs a man square in the heart.

It is the grip of fear that ensnares his entire waking moment.

It is the image that fills the entire screen of his mind.

When he finally realizes that he is going to Die!

Until we learn this, life is an endless stream of events. Until we learn this, we will live within the illusion of an

Abundance Of Time. And that which is in abundance is Never valued.

Nature should be more kind to man. It should subject man to a near-death experience at least once every six months. Just to remind him that His Time Is Running Out.

To remind him that this paper existence that he lives is about to Whither. To remind him not to get too comfortable. To remind him not to take his life seriously, for it is only on Lease. To remind him that every "grand achievement" and every bit of respectability and every drop of his so-called reputation is Going To Fall As Common Dust.

It is said that Alexander The Great once met an Indian sage who asked him, "Alexander, what if you were walking in the desert, dying of thirst, and I had a bottle of water? What would you be prepared to give me for that bottle of water?"

To which Alexander replied, "I would be willing to give half my kingdom for that bottle of water."

The Indian sage said, "What if that deal was not acceptable to me?"

Alexander said, "Then I would be willing to give you my entire kingdom."

The Indian sage replied, "You are a very silly man. Devoting your entire life to waging wars and conquering lands. All for a bottle of water."

We are even sillier than Alexander. For at least Alexander

had a life-and-death excuse for craving the bottle of water.

We have refrigerators full of water, yet we waste our lives seeking an extra drop.

Why do we do this?

Because our situation is not as clear to us as it was for Alexander. Alexander knew precisely what he craved. He knew exactly what he was thirsty for.

The sage's question had defined the problem so perfectly for him, that the solution became clear.

Our problem is that although we thirst, we do not know what exactly we are thirsting for. As a result, we wander through life grasping at shiny and colorful things hoping to quench our thirst. But the things we find never do the job.

The paths that we walk are circular rather than linear. And as a result, we go nowhere.

The elixirs we drink are filled with salt. And thus we remain thirsty. The dreams we have do often materialize, but then they lead only to more dreams.

We cry in the quiet of our room. Wondering how to escape from our plight. And the more we attempt to escape from it, the more we become ensnared by it.

The lonely and thirsty wanderer in the desert is in a far more enviable situation, is he not? His life is simple. He has only one need. And once he gets it, he is content.

But may that man never leave the desert. Though he may not realize it, the bare open expanse of desert is his only

salvation.

Why?

Because if he trades the wilds of the desert for the paved roads of civilized life, his life will become immediately more complex. Where he once had only one need, he will now have hundreds.

Where he once thirsted only for water, he will now thirst for everything under creation. And in doing so, he will become a far more pitiful creature than he ever was in the desert.

Life made a mistake with human beings. It overestimated our ability to see The Truth.

The truth is that we are only here for a short while. Yet the calendar on the wall displays days from here until eternity. The watch winds up instead of down. This is complete deception, is it not?

The only worthwhile watch in the world is not the one which counts Up, but the one which counts Down.

Not the watch which tells you what time It Is. But the watch which tells you how much time you Have Left.

To know the very day that you are going to die. And to have a watch which tells you how much time remains in your life. That is a life-changing watch!

Unless we have a watch like this . . .

Unless we have a multitude of near-death experiences . . .

Unless we Viscerally come face to face with our own

demise . . .

We will never know death.

And if we never have the luxury of knowing death, we will forever suffer the misery of not having lived.

Of What Use Is A Birth Certificate?

May I ask you a question?

Of what use is a birth certificate?

Such a certificate only encourages human beings. It encourages us to believe in infinity. It encourages us to believe that we have been granted an unending stream of years whose end is simply incomprehensible.

If a birth date needs to be documented, write it on the living room wall.

But the thing of value, the embossed certificate, should not state something so obvious as the time of birth.

What it should state, in bold black letters with a font greater than every other word on the page is the **Time Of Your Impending Death**!

To know the day you are going to die from the very moment you are born . . .

To know what you have to work with . . .

To know exactly how much time you have . . .

If you knew this, you would never be faced with having to get your affairs in order. For they would never have been disordered to begin with.

Perhaps you would not allow yourself to luxuriate in your emotional indulgences. The shrinkage of time into a manageable sum would allow you to plan. It would allow you to not waste time.

It would allow you to live.

Death is the greatest motivator. And what a wonderful friend it would be to our existence. Because we feel we have so much time, we waste it by the truckload. We have no value for the day. We fail to understand that this day will never come again.

This is because we see today as yesterday. And we will see tomorrow as today.

And thus our life moves. With us constantly being a step behind. Smiling toward an empty hope. Believing in a seemingly endless future.

Dying is common. Living is an outright scarcity.

He who believes in death, will soon begin to revere life.

He who believes in tomorrow, will have no value for today.

The Sky Is Absolutely, Positively Falling

The most cataclysmic mistake of your entire life is believing that you have time.

You have become so incredibly comfortable in this well-worn life of yours. There is an oval depression right in the center of it, where you nestle into it.

There is so little time. But you are so accustomed to hearing from science fiction movies that tell you that the end is coming that you have become numb to it.

Intellectually, you Know that you are only here for a short time. You Know that your days are numbered. But intellectual knowing is only good for Trivial Pursuit. Intellectual knowing does not change your life.

Do you know that your days are numbered?

You will likely reply with a reflexive and meaningless "yes."

But if you truly know that your days are numbered, how many days do you think you have left? How many years? How many months?

If I tell you that you might have Zero days left . . .

If it tell you that you might die Tomorrow, you will acknowledge this with that matter-of-fact Knowing. You will probably even be thinking of something else while answering the question.

And this is the way it is going to be until death comes to you.

You will die with unsettled affairs. Fixing your curtains, making your bed, and mending the loose ends of your comfortable life.

Your mind says that for you it will be different. That you

are special. Your mind will ask you, "Do you really believe that you are going to die tomorrow?" It will tell you that you have plenty of time. It will tell you that your most important duty right now is to save for retirement. To refinance your house. To re-upholster that comfortable couch. To fix the dent on the car.

As I said, you are completely immersed in this life of yours. And that is why it will be such a gargantuan shock when death arrives.

This death is a funny thing. It always comes at the most inopportune times. It does not even have the decency to make an appointment or wait until it is convenient.

It's coming. It has already started its journey Straight Toward You.

You don't believe me?

Is there any shortage of death around you? Are people not dying everywhere? Every hour? Every single day?

And for Every One of those people, Death Came Too Soon. It rudely came before the time was right. They needed more time. But it ripped through their life in a flash.

I won't try to convince you that the sky is falling. I will simply tell you that it is.

I know you won't believe me. Your mind will dismiss my words. It will bring your attention back to planning the next thirty years of your life.

You look at your life and you see an endless horizon. You see an endless amount of time.

And this one fact more than any other prevents your life from exploding into bliss.

The Path To Atmamun

If you knew that you were going to die tomorrow, today would be the most blissful day of your life.

All things would immediately explode into perspective. The insignificant elements of your life would immediately drop away. Because you would no longer have the luxury of time.

Man is by nature an eleventh hour creature. It is only when he is threatened with everything that he decides to do anything.

Break through the illusion that you have time. See all of the names in the obituaries and the cemeteries and KNOW that YOU are next!

This will pluck you from your complacency. And force you to look at the things in your life that are most immediate and most in need of attention.

Is there anything more important in your life than living in bliss?

Then understand that time is not your friend.

Understand that you have a finite number of breaths left in your lungs.

And with each passing one, you come closer to death.
We are all quite literally DYING.
And this more than anything else will keep us close to LIFE.

ALL CONFLICT IS SELF-CONFLICT

You have never in your life had a single conflict with another human being.

Never!

Our behaviors are a manifestation of our internal state. Our state of being. Our state of understanding. Our state of ignorance. Our state of wisdom.

That which the world has categorized as "natural" is not natural at all. It is a conditioned response. And because everyone around you has the same conditioned responses, you consider it to be "natural."

Conflict is at the center of all of our lives. It is such a ubiquitous element of our lives that it is perhaps the greatest reason for our lack of joy.

When people seek help for conflict, it is typically in the form of "conflict resolution." Essentially, they are asking for tips and remedies by which to Undo the tangled web. And they are given exactly that. They are given Prescriptions for what to say and how to look at things from the other person's perspective and how to be more empathetic and patient and understanding.

It is a form of behavior modification. And when one hears it, it sounds perfectly reasonable. And while doing this may lessen the frequency of conflict, it often comes back full force. For conflict is so pervasive in our lives that most wouldn't even consider seeking "help" for it.

When someone says something hurtful to us, we react in anger outwardly and feel pain inwardly. Advisors tell them that they have the right to feel angry, but to modify the response.

My dear friend, looking at things in this way is the reason that you have been putting out fires all of your life. And you will continue to grapple with thousands more.

Why?

Because you have been too eager for solutions. You have been so quick to jump to the "answer" that you haven't asked the question.

Let us take anger as an example. If someone calls you an idiot, you get angry.

You have spent your entire life asking how to overcome the anger. Or to modify your response to the insult. Or to take deep breaths. Or to repeat a mantra. Or to wait ten minutes before responding.

> But the true solution to this problem lies in asking a completely different question. And the question is this: If someone insults me, what is the reason that anger arises in me?

Not how to "deal with" it. Or how to lessen it. Or how to

eradicate it.

But to understand why it arises in the first place.

Anger is not a form of self-defense. It is a manifestation of inner conflict.

And understand this: ALL Conflict Is Self-Conflict.

You need not worry about the other. You need not attempt to change the other. You need not make the other see your way. You need not the apology of the other.

Why?

Because There Is No Other!

You see, if someone calls you an idiot, something within you at least partially entertains or accepts the idea that you are an idiot. This idea that you may be an idiot, in turn, causes you to feel very uneasy about yourself. And this uneasiness is manifested as anger.

The person calling you an idiot simply set the stage and created the opportunity for you to examine how you felt about yourself. And when you did not like what you saw internally, you reacted with anger externally.

The anger, in this example, is simply a manifestation of the inner conflict of entertaining the possibility that you are an idiot and disliking the fact that you are entertaining it in the first place.

I will state categorically that if within yourself there was no possibility that you were an idiot, anger simply would not arise.

The Path To Atmamun

We believe that our responses are to people and situations. And the reason that we believe this is because of the temporal relationship between the response and the inciting person or event.

But in understanding that our emotional responses come from entertaining the possibility that the criticism is valid, we will begin to examine the source of this self-criticism, rather than the source which provoked the emotional response.

If we understand that the mind levels undue criticism by its very nature, we will begin to discover the root of the problem.

If we come to terms with our own strengths and misgivings, we cannot be bothered by anyone or anything.

And imagine what your life would be like if you learned to live in this way.

THE RICH MAN'S GREATEST LUXURY

The bible says that it is easier for a camel to go through the eye of a needle than it is for a rich man to enter the kingdom of God.

I believe this to be a statement which unfairly targets the rich. For what this statement is fundamentally speaking of is Attachment.

The rich do not have a monopoly on attachment. The man with little to no money is just as attached to his meager possessions as the rich man is to his luxurious ones.

Virtually all of my clients are extraordinarily wealthy. They can afford all of society's pleasures. They can satisfy their every wish. They can fulfill their every desire.

But the reason that they have come to me is to Experience the one thing that money has not been able to buy them.

And that thing is **FREEDOM. Freedom from the torment of the mind. Freedom to feel bliss and equanimity on the inside, regardless of what his happening on the outside.**

The ability to devote their life to the attainment of Freedom and Bliss is, in fact, their greatest luxury.

You see, the poor man has no time to fill his soul. For his

first priority is to fill his stomach.

The rich man's possessions afford him convenience and luxury, but these are not his true riches. For they leave him empty for something more.

The rich man's appetite is great. For his entire life, this appetite has been directed toward success, achievement, and accumulation. And at a certain time in his life, after he has water skied behind his yachts and taken his numerous trips around the world in his private jet, he begins to ask certain questions.

He is confronted by the limitations of his wealth. And, perhaps for the first time in his life, he turns his direction toward that which remains after he has exhausted all of his luxuries and indulgences.

He finds that the greatest luxury that his wealth has afforded him is the luxury to turn inward. To devote his time and his energies toward tasting the nectar of life.

The appetite that allowed him to succeed in his craft now allows him to succeed in life's ultimate journey: The journey toward his true nature.

The dogged determination that served him in his craft, now serves him in his journey toward Truth. He has lived as a King of men. And now he must learn to live as the King of himself.

The irony is that once a man achieves Atmamun, he is able to enjoy his possessions infinitely more. He is able to perform his craft at an exponential level. He is able to truly enjoy the relationships that are valuable to him, and deftly

handle those that are not.

Why?

Because for the first time in his life, he is attached to none of it.

Through Atmamun, he has become Free. He holds his empire loosely. And in doing so, he does not suffer the weight of its presence.

This is his final frontier. This is his Everest.

And upon summiting it, he truly becomes the God he was always meant to be.

The Path To Atmamun

Understand that your wealth is not a house that you walk into, but a scaffolding that you must climb. For as long as you are attached to it, you will be owned by it.

Do not pay heed to those who ask you to give it all away and live in poverty. For attachment to poverty is just as imprisoning as an attachment to wealth.

Now that you have attained success and accumulation, there is one final journey that you must embark upon if you wish to taste true Freedom.

The empire that you have built is sitting on your shoulders. The solution is not to rid yourself of it, but to simply get out from underneath it. For it is only then that you will be able to enjoy it.

Take advantage of the single greatest luxury that your wealth has afforded you.

Embark upon the path to Atmamun, and you will become as Rich as a living God.

BECOME THE GOD OF YOUR OWN LIFE

You've done wretched things in your life.

You've unfairly treated those you love. You've abused your authority. You've lied in bed with unbearable guilt over the thoughts you've had and the behaviors you've allowed yourself to succumb to.

You haven't been a role model to your children. You haven't been a true companion to your spouse.

Simply put, you've become a person you never thought you would become.

I understand, my dear friend.

We are all wretched in so many ways. We lose our way easily in this world. We lose ourselves to the mind and we carry out its bidding. It is in many ways the human condition.

Understand that every holy man was once a wretched man. Every man of wisdom was once a man of ignorance. And he lived so consistently with ignorance that one day the ignorance became so unbearable it was time to let it go.

This is not about changing behavior. For behavior is the natural consequence of the degree to which we live within the mind.

I won't give you a motivational speech and tell you that things will change. They haven't changed in thirty, forty, or fifty years. In fact, things have only gotten worse.

Why would they change now?

Water boils at 100 degrees Celsius. At 99 degrees it only simmers. Are you at 100? Or are you at 99?

Mind you, I'm not attempting to get you to 100. The question is a sincere one.

If you are at 99, my words will resonate, but they will not transform. If you are at 100, my words will catalyze your transformation.

There are people in this world who live as saints. People who have discovered the true beauty in life. People who live in constant peace. And endless joy.

Can you become one of them?

If this is the question you are asking, then the answer is No. For the person who wonders if something is possible remains tied to impossibility.

The reason that you are the way you are is because, on some level, it is okay with you to be the way you are.

To give yourself the permission to be the way you are, and also the freedom to lament about it is a great luxury. And it is a luxury that will never allow you to know life.

Change is cosmetic. For he who changes, changes back.

Transformation is permanent. And it begins with a decision.

Not a decision to acquire, but a decision to lose.

What about yourself would you like to lose? What are the things in your life and outlook that you would like to completely abandon?

I will warn you. It will not be easy. For you are emotionally tied to your destructive habits. You are enmeshed within them. And as you tear away the habits, you will also tear away parts of yourself.

And while you will certainly rejoice at seeing the habits go, will you also rejoice at seeing those parts of you float away?

My friend, you will not get a true feel of the ocean with one foot firmly on the sand. You must dive into the depths. Become saturated with the new possibility. And it is only then that you will acquire a new skin.

To become the human being you've always wanted to be, you must be willing to walk away from the human being you've become.

When preservation is of no consequence . . .

When self-protection has no meaning . . .

When Instant Transformation is your single-minded goal . . .

It will happen to you.

You will look into the mirror and see a new face. You will see the world through new eyes. You will behave differently without having attempted to change your behavior.

To walk away from your image of yourself is the most difficult and painful journey in the world.

But without it you will never know bliss.

Bliss is known in emptiness rather than form. It is

heralded by mystery rather than familiarity. The only man who can walk this path is the one who is willing to lose everything.

How can a man be willing to lose everything?

When he realizes that all that he has is not what he has truly been seeking. And when he realizes this, it immediately becomes okay to lose it.

Just for that one chance to acquire what his heart has always wanted.

Just for that one chance to become the human being you've always wanted to be.

Just for that once chance to become the God Of Your Own Life.

The Path To Atmamun

The Path to Atmamun is the path to becoming your own God.

If everything outside of a man does not happen according to him, everything on the inside can indeed go according to him. This awaits the man who becomes his own God.

To remain untouched by anything that happens in the world. This awaits the man who becomes his own God.

To face any conflict and hold it at arm's length. This awaits the man who becomes his own God.

To produce a masterpiece with every action that he pursues. This awaits the man who becomes his own God.

Nature is Natural. Nature is Perfect. Nature is Pure. Nature is Whole. Nature suffers zero turmoil. And lives in complete serenity.

Nature is a living, breathing masterpiece.

I ask you pointedly: Is this not the way that you should be?

I ask you honestly: Do you deserve anything less?

About the Author

I was born in Northern India. Not far from the foothills of the Himalayas.

When I was a boy I was captivated by the stories of the Himalayan sadhus. Their understanding of life. Their investigation of the human mind. Their unparalleled insights into the ways of nature. Their achievement of true bliss.

I spent years reading the ancient texts, listening to modern gurus, reading ancient folklore, and watching lectures on video. And after many years of searching in this way, what I discovered was that they all said the same things.

And listening to their words did nothing to quench my thirst for The Truth.

The one authentic man . . .

The one who inspired me beyond compare . . .

Was Siddhartha Gautama (The Buddha).

He set off on a search for Truth. To the know the Ultimate Reality. To see with his very own eyes. And when he ventured into the dense forests of Northern India, he came across ascetics whom he began to follow.

And soon he came to the very same conclusion that I had: These people had not found Truth. They were no more evolved than him.

It is then that he realized that there was only one journey that could lead him to his destination. And this was The

Personal Journey. Without teachers, swamis, or scriptures.

And in doing so, he arrived at a place within himself that few in the history of civilization ever have.

After his death, his words were documented into scriptures and books. And while his story is nothing short of inspirational, his message has become lost.

For what he found cannot be experienced through "noble truths." It can only be experienced through DIRECT EXPERIENCE.

The man who conquered his mind and came to know his true nature did so precisely because he Did Not follow doctrine. Yet, ironically, his words have been turned into doctrine.

And just as "words" did not help him, they do not, in my experience, help anyone.

I have spent decades on my Journey toward The Truth. I have done my own experiments related to the true nature of Mind. I have followed the emotional energies back to their source. I have investigated the human being at his deepest core.

And I have come up with Truths that have had Transformative effects upon my life, and those clients who serendipity has brought my way.

I am not a guru or a swami. And I preach no religion. For religion has nothing to do with God.

Man Is God. In every sense of the word.

My way of working with human beings has little to do with prescriptions, or meditation, or yoga.

My way is to help the human being find himself.

My way is to help the human being find what he has always been in search of, whether he realized it or not: COMPLETE and UNBRIDLED FREEDOM.

Once a human being finds this, he is not in need of any "teaching." For he becomes his own master.

ATMAMUN is a process I have developed over two decades. It is actually a non-teaching. A path away from all paths.

It allows the human being to transcend his mind. And become God himself.

And once he does, he bears a new skin, and sees through different eyes.

He Experiences the world directly.

He experiences it as only a Free Man can.

Atmamun is the path to achieve the bliss of the Himalayan swamis. And the Freedom of a living God.

— Kapil Gupta, MD

Siddha Performance

Dr. Gupta is also the founder of *Siddha Performance*.

He has applied his work on the human mind to the world of performance in professional sports and business.

He has discovered training methods which are based solely upon Perception rather than technique.

Perception training is a form of SUPER-TRAINING. It allows an individual to achieve exponential results in a fraction of the time normally required.

This allows him to OWN his craft.

Whether it is a professional athlete, a world class executive, or an elite performing artist, understanding his mind through the process of Atmamun allows him to be completely free of anxiety. And live in Total Clarity.

His work can be found at *www.SiddhaPerformance.com*

Websites and Media

For worldwide speaking engagements, corporate training, or correspondence . . .

Dr. Gupta can be reached via his websites:

www.KapilGuptaMD.com
and
www.SiddhaPerformance.com

He has written numerous discourses on these websites and print publications, including others such as ***Tiny Buddha, Lifehack, Dumb Little Man, Elephant Journal, High Existence, and Common Ground Magazine.***

He has also served as a regular contributor to the ***On The Mark*** show with Mark Immelman on PGA Tour Radio.

Twitter: @KapilGuptaMD

Facebook: www.facebook/KapilGuptaMD

Facebook Fan Page: https://www.facebook.com/Kapil-Gupta-MD-1435690079979645/

Atmamun

Atmamun

Printed in Poland
by Amazon Fulfillment
Poland Sp. z o.o., Wrocław

54900148R00110

In any discipline, in any nation, the prevailing logic is essentially Noise. This noise satisfies the disinterested and the slightly curious. But it frustrates the passionate and the serious.

The disciplines of personal growth, self-help, and spirituality are saturated with bumper-sticker slogans such as happiness, positive-thinking, meditation, and mindfulness. These have been institutionalized. And they represent the Noise of this domain.

Such concepts may lend a dose of incremental change. But rarely do they lead to Transformation. They may provide a boost in mood, but rarely do they lead to Freedom.

This book contains the insights that few in the history of civilization have ever Truly Experienced. But those who have, became living Gods.

This is the book for that One True Seeker. It is for that Rare One who seeks to live a life of Unbridled Freedom. And to live his life as the God he was created to be.

This is ATMAMUN.

Dr. Gupta has spent more than two decades developing the process of Atmamun as a path by which to gain mastery over the human mind and attain True Freedom in one's life.

Dr. Gupta's clients include elite professional athletes, celebrities, and world class executives. Dr. Gupta guides them through the process of Atmamun in order to help them become the God of their own lives.

ISBN 9781532762727